Henry Stacy Marks

Pen And Pencil Sketches Marks

Vol. II.

Henry Stacy Marks

Pen And Pencil Sketches Marks
Vol. II.

ISBN/EAN: 9783337009557

Printed in Europe, USA, Canada, Australia, Japan

Cover: Foto ©Thomas Meinert / pixelio.de

More available books at **www.hansebooks.com**

PEN AND PENCIL SKETCHES

VOL. II

The Old Clock.

From the Original Picture belonging to W.ᵐ J. W. Haigh of Ledsham.

PEN AND PENCIL SKETCHES ❋❋❋ By HENRY STACY MARKS R.A. ❋❋❋

IN TWO VOLUMES

VOL. II

London

CHATTO & WINDUS, PICCADILLY

1894

Printed by BALLANTYNE, HANSON & CO.
At the Ballantyne Press

CONTENTS

CHAPTER XIV

ART CRITIC AND CONTRIBUTOR TO THE "SPECTATOR"

CHAPTER XVII

A PUGILIST PAINTER

CHAPTER XVIII

ILLUSTRATED PAPERS AND ARTISTS' PICTURE SUNDAY

CHAPTER XIX

LONDON

CHAPTER XX

MODELS

CHAPTER XXI

BAMPTON

CHAPTER XXII

BIRDS—THE ZOO

CHAPTER XXIII

RUSKIN

CHAPTER XXIV

THE HORSE—THE DOG

The question of respective popularity—The brute man—The
horse and the chough—Military tournaments—Horse-racing
and betting—The three-card trick—"He was but a landscape painter"—Scene on Lewes racecourse—The somewhat debasing influence of "horse"—Horsey men—The
life of the horse—Has he a future?—"If for the tyrant shall
it be denied the slave?"—An appalling confession—"I
loathe and detest the dog"—Literature and Art have com-
bined to glorify him—Lord Byron's "one friend," a Newfoundland dog—Dogs and dogs—The dog and the doctor
—The dog the master—Woman and *her* master, the disgusting toy or lap-dog—Dog stories—"Binkie," the pet-dog

CHAPTER XXVII

BOOK-PLATES, OR "EX LIBRIS"

LIST OF ILLUSTRATIONS

IN VOL. II

PEN AND PENCIL SKETCHES

CHAPTER XIV

ART CRITIC AND CONTRIBUTOR TO THE "SPECTATOR"

Shorteared, (Rili.

I N looking over the series of articles I wrote more than thirty years ago for the *Spectator*, with the signature of "Dry-point," it occurred to me that some of them, or some portions of them, might be interesting to the general reader. I do not propose to inflict my critical views of that period upon him to any extent. Those views would now be deemed old-fashioned and out of date ; and though in many cases expressed with the fearless boldness of youth, would be regarded as tame and commonplace compared with the incisive and dog-matic dicta of the apostles of the "new" criticism of

the hour—dicta which are final, and from which
there is and shall be no appeal. But if I give at
greater length articles of a general and more descriptive nature, I have unearthed some few critical
remarks which are not without interest, even if it
be antiquarian, and of which I give the following
as a sample.

It seems difficult now to imagine the work of the
President of the Royal Academy being badly hung,
yet I find in my notice of the Exhibition of 1861
this remonstrance with the arrangers of that
year :—

"Much of Mr. F. Leighton's work this year is
replete with great beauty. In poetic feeling, the
refinements of drawing, harmony of lines, in composition, and general balance of parts, he may
safely challenge comparison with any English
painter. 128 is a portrait of a lady in black bonnet
and dress, very masterly in drawing, modelling,
and expression. 'Capri' (645) shows what can
be done by this artist in landscape. But it is in
'Lieder ohne Worte' (550) that Mr. Leighton's
powers are seen in perfection. The picture of a
girl reclining in an attitude of voluptuous and
dreamy indolence by a white marble fountain, the
stillness only broken by the gurgling of the limpid
water and the song of the bird, is a masterpiece
of refinement. It has its faults, but its charms in

spite of them. One returns to it again and again with renewed pleasure. It is not perhaps within a critic's province to speak of picture *frames*, yet I cannot help drawing attention to that which surrounds this work. The pure taste and inventiveness which it displays would almost imply that the painter had a hand in its design. *The hangers have not been guilty of a crueller act this year than that of placing this beautiful picture at a height where its merits can be only partially seen."*

In March 1862 the most important picture sale of the season at Christie's was that of the collection of Mr. Thomas E. Plint of Liverpool, which included many of the most celebrated works by the Pre-Raphaelites, of which school Mr. Plint was a great admirer. One of the choicest examples was the "Carpenter's Shop" by Millais, painted and exhibited only a dozen years previously, when it evoked a storm of abuse of the most virulent kind, not only from the press, but from the general body of painters. I am glad to think, from the lines which follow, that I felt I could honestly say a good word for that much-derided picture :—

"Mr. Millais's 'Carpenter's Shop' is one of the chief attractions, and deservedly so ; for though first exhibited twelve years ago, it contains passages of painting never yet surpassed by the artist. Who does not recollect the howl of criticism raised against this picture by the press during the Exhibition of 1850? In vain I looked for the sores, the varicose veins, and other abominations which the imaginative critics of the day declared to be therein set forth. Asceticism of treatment, the fallacy of selecting the coarsest types of humanity as actors in a scriptural scene, are palpable enough; yet, with all its errors, it is a work of the rarest power. The flesh painting is marvellous in its truth of tone and purity of colour; it does not suffer by imme-diate comparison with one's own wrist or palm. The drawing, if hard, is strong and accurate, and in some of the extremities particularly, approaches very nearly to perfection. The expressions of the heads are intensified to the highest pitch, and the execution, though wonderfully finished and elaborate, has nowhere the appearance of labour. The little St. John is the most pleasing conception in the group, and atones by his graceful, natural attitude and innocent face for the vulgarity of form and feature observable in the other figures. It is a wonderful work, rendered still more wonderful by the reflection that it was wrought by the brain and hand of a lad not twenty years of age."

It is satisfactory to reflect that this judgment has been since confirmed by wiser heads and abler pens than my own.

I pass over all other references to pictures in the famous Plint sale, but cannot resist quoting the following, which in its title affords a delightful specimen of unconscious humour : — "A name I have not met with before is appended to a production so singularly bad that it is to be hoped that it will be a long time before we again hear of Mr. B. P. Marshall. Its lengthy and curious title is worth quoting, however : 'George Stephenson modelling engines in clay—first thoughts of the locomotive, his wife, who died young, and a favourite rabbit !' "

Here are a couple of tiny notices, one of which proved to be prophetical :—"A little picture called 'Mist on the Moors,' a girl driving a couple of calves, by Mr. G. Mason (a new name), is noticeable for a truthful action and graceful arrangement of lines that suggest Continental study.

"A name new to me is appended to a pair of little pictures, unpretending in subject, but evincing great pictorial aptitude. The first, with the ill-chosen title of 'Jotted Down,' is the better of the two : a little girl is seated in a meadow, and crying over a basket of sticks overturned by two boys, who scamper off in the distance. There is a quaint pathos in the action of the child, and the landscape is unaffectedly realistic. 'La Voisine' is an old woman knocking at a door. Both pictures are somewhat

French in style, and promise well for the future success of Mr. G. H. Boughton."

And to conclude, I give my first criticism on my friend Walker, taken from a review of "an illustrated gift-book : "—" Mr. F. Walker is a young artist who has already earned a high reputation among his brethren, and cannot fail to take a good stand in public estimation. His drawings are full of tender feeling and unaffected nature. The subject of a child praying at its mother's knee has been often done, but Mr. Walker contrives to make the old story new, not by any striving after originality, but simply from his artless manner of telling it."

In my capacity of art critic to the *Spectator* I was allowed perfect freedom in choice of subject, never had my articles cut down or interfered with, and corrections, if any, seldom extended beyond one or two words. The article here given in its entirety is a proof that my editors were very lenient, and allowed me to interpret art in the broadest possible sense :—

" There must be few who have not had, in their boyish days, a passion for the purchase and illumination of those singular theatrical prints still occasionally to be seen in toyshop windows, and known as Skelt's or Park's 'favourite characters.' Many will recollect hoarding their pocket-money from week to week to save sufficient wherewith to pur-

chase the tinsel, satin, and spangles requisite for
the complete glorification of 'Mr. Smith as the
Pirate of the Dark Blue Waters,' 'Mr. Kean as
Richard III.,' or devoting their winter evenings to
essays in water-colour, which the clear light of day
frequently pronounced to be failures, by showing
that under the influence of artificial light we had
not unnaturally mistaken our colours, and painted
skies green and trees blue, while the complexion
of a domestic heroine, which at night appeared of
an interesting and delicate pallor, seemed in the
morning to have suffered considerably from an
attack of yellow jaundice. Some, more ambitious,
aspired to the management of a miniature theatre,
and great was the amount of time devoted to cutting
out the figures from the plates of 'Park's Characters'
and 'Scenes in the Miller and his Men,' colouring
them, mounting them on cardboard, fitting the
stage with curtain, footlights, and proscenium,
and, when all was ready, inviting one's friends to
witness the representation of the unexciting melo-
drama. The pasteboard characters were pushed on
to the stage in little tin slides, and made their exits
and entrances with becoming gravity. The manager,
generally actor as well, read the parts from the
prompt-book behind the stage, and it was curious
to notice the great similarity of voice possessed
by the *dramatis personæ*; how in their wildest

moments of passion they would yet conduct themselves with due decorum, and go through a scene of some minutes' duration in a fixed and rigid attitude not pleasant to behold. There were many hitches in the performance; the wrong actor often appeared at the wrong moment and in the wrong place; something was generally faulty about the scenery, and there was considerable delay in getting the red fire, which was to destroy the bad genius of the piece at the conclusion of the drama, to burn. Still much amusement was extracted upon these occasions; and though one's recollection of these juvenile performances may not be very cheering to look back upon, the reflection occurs, that it is possible even now-a-days to witness theatrical representations on a larger stage, and with living actors, that can scarcely be considered more entertaining.

"Of the antiquity of the production of the theatrical character plates, I am unable to offer very precise data, but believe that they were unknown before the commencement of this or the latter end of last century. The originator of them was a Mr. West, who for many years kept open a shop devoted to their sale in Wych Street, opposite the Olympic Theatre. Skelt and Park followed, the latter of whom has, perhaps, the largest existing business in theatrical and Twelfth-Night characters, valentines, cheap coloured lithographs, and song-books. But the trade in theatrical characters is unfortunately rapidly declining, owing partly to the number of cheap illustrated periodicals now published, and partly, perhaps, to the rapid strides of that educational movement of which so much is heard at the present day. Whether or no, the fact remains the same; no new plates are issued, as the demand for them would not repay the cost of production, and when the old plates have become too worn to yield further impressions, it is possible that our 'favourite characters' will become things of the past. The figures are engraved on plates of copper and steel, with deeply incised lines, so as to produce as large a number of copies as possible, and it is to be hoped the contingency hinted at above may be remote; but it would be as well for antiquarians to pay a visit to Leonard Street, Finsbury, at once, and procure specimens of the works which may one day be regarded with curiosity if not admiration. The expense attendant on such a course will not be heavy. 'Mr. G. Honner as the Fire King,' or 'St. George and the Dragon,' may be obtained at the low rate of a penny each 'plain,' or 'twopence coloured;' and a book of the words of a popular play, with the six plates of characters, eight scenes, and four wings necessary for its effective representation, may be purchased for thirteenpence.

"In the early days of Pre-Raphaelitism, when the young disciples of the new creed were hotly enthusiastic, and believed they were about to revolutionise the world of art, when they called Reynolds 'Sir Sloshy Kennels,' ridiculed the old masters, and hung the copies which they had made (in unenlightened days) from Titian and Rubens upside down as a mark of contempt, they also compared 'Park's favourite characters' with Raphael's cartoons, slightly to the disadvantage of the latter. Without wishing to endorse an opinion to which probably the Pre-Raphaelites who uttered it would scarcely adhere in their wiser days, I may state that between the art of Park and that of the ancient Egyptians, or even that of the Greeks, there are many points of affinity. That mechanical regularity of proportion in the limbs, that conventional treatment of form, and that limited variety of attitude, which are the chief characteristics of the works of the Egyptian artist, will be found also in Park's figures. The Greek, ever aiming at abstract beauty of form, seldom attempted to realise marked facial expression. With the exception of the Dying Gladiator and the Laocoon, there are scarcely any known antiques which depict violent emotion. The faces are generally calm and passionless. So it is with Park ; the slightest possible contraction of the brow is deemed sufficient for the portrayal of grief, rage,

or terror. We find but few traces of humour in
the art of Egypt or of Greece; nor is it a quality
exemplified in a high degree by Park. I can find
no higher example than is afforded by giving a
very rotund paunch to Falstaff, or a pair of knock-
knees and a button-like nose to a clown. Such
are the principal points of resemblance discoverable
between the monuments of antiquity and the works
of Park, but a strong dissimilarity will be discovered
in the fact, that whereas in the former energetic
action is seldom seen, in the latter it becomes a
prominent feature. As Demosthenes considered
action to be the prime element in oratory, so Park
holds it to be the one thing needful in dramatic
art. His figures are always in violent attitudes.
That which occurs most frequently is a kind of
tragic start, obtained by throwing the whole weight
of the body on one leg, and stretching out the other
as far as it will go. One hand must point defiantly
to an imaginary object, the other must grasp a
cutlass, a pair of pistols, or anything else that is
convenient and looks bloodthirsty. The cast of
features is in all cases pretty much the same. The
face of a doll, black staring eyes, strongly corked
eyebrows and moustache, and aquiline nose, small
mouth, and a profusion of dark ringlets (fair hair
is out of the question), are given alike to the
'Green Knight' or the 'Demon of the Deep.'

Small feet and well-developed calves are also much dwelt upon, and other peculiarities might be noticed. Thus pistols are always carried at full cock whether in the hand or in the belt—the belt is found also to be a more convenient means for the stowage of purses than the capacious pockets of the Jack Sheppard era. The highwayman always wears a laced cocked-hat, gilt epaulettes, ruffles, and Life Guards' boots. The pirate embroiders his garments with the perennial skull and marrow-bones, and wears the sailor's large shirt-collar and loose handkerchief of to-day over a brazen corselet of no particular period whatever. The ethereal nature of the fairy is expressed by a more than wasp-like thinness of waist, and the insect character is further enhanced by a pair of butterfly wings. St. George, in an odd mixture of nudity and scale armour, fights with a small green dragon. The sword which our patron saint holds is so short, and the horse he rides so tall, that it is problematical how he will ever get a cut at his enemy without dismounting to finish the combat on foot. This plate is the most popular ever published, and it is no uncommon thing to see it hanging up in a neat black frame and enveloped with all the glories tinsel can bestow upon it in the homes of the London poorer classes. A plate containing a number of little portraits of European celebrities is not without a certain unconscious fun. By it we find that the Empress of the French does *not* wear her hair in the style which she is popularly supposed have originated, but in ringlets ; that Sir Colin Campbell is a beardless youth, wearing scarf and trews of tartan ; and that Sir Charles Napier has at length followed the moustache movement. The landscapes which form the subjects of some of the scenes from plays are drawn with great freedom, if not with much truth or knowledge. A uniform touch expresses foliage or sea-foam with equally pleasing results ; houses and other build-ings are drawn in noble defiance of perspective law ; the specimens of rock-drawing would scarcely satisfy the critical acumen of Mr. Ruskin, nor would he greatly prefer the ramification of stem and branch in ' Park's new tree wings ' to the ' india-rubber boughs ' of Gaspar Poussin.

" The ' Juvenile Dramas written for Park's char-acters and scenes in the same,' are chiefly melo-dramatic. The works of Shakespeare, though they have been tortured in many ways, find no place in the Parkian drama. The ' Miller and his Men ' is more in request than any other of the plays. Next in favour is the ' Red Rover ; '—' Der Frei-schutz ; ' ' Blue Beard ' and ' Jack Sheppard ' also enjoy extensive popularity. In the adaptation of these dramas from the original plays much license

is taken, and it is more than probable the author
would scarcely recognise his work in its later form.
The plot is, in most cases, obscure, strikingly im-
probable, and deficient in constructive skill. The
personages perform acts for which it would be
difficult to assign motives, and when you expect
them to be going to do one thing, they invariably
do the exact opposite. These trifling defects are
in some measure remedied by the stirring incidents
of the action; the young mind cares little for the
dramatic unities, provided there be a tolerable
amount of fighting and blue fire. The dialogue
can scarcely be considered sparkling in its wit, or
thrilling from the intensity of passion it conveys.
Thus in Scene i. Act 2, of the 'Red Rover,'
which takes place on the main-deck of the pirate
vessel, the Rover enters to Madame de Lacy and
Gertrude, and the following brilliant conversation
ensues :

"'*Rover*. Good morning, ladies. I dare say you think
our lives a very dull one.

"'*Madame*. On the contrary, sir, *nothing can be more
delightful than to witness the setting of the sun on the
ocean.*

"'*Rover*. Perhaps the young lady would like to witness
a little sport with the crew on deck ; I have no doubt but
what some of my men will amuse you.'

Whereupon an energetic hornpipe is performed

by some of the sailors, but we are left in doubt as
to whether the young lady is amused or bored.
She offers no opinion or thanks for the performance, being, indeed, of a very impassive nature, for
she opens her mouth only four times during the
entire play."

The above article is a pretty good proof that I
was allowed perfect liberty, a liberty which, in
this instance, all but degenerated into license. Yet
it only provoked a grave but kindly remonstrance
in the shape of a brief note from one of the
editors warning me that readers might have *too*
much banter! So I became grave, and carefully
laid aside the cap and bells for a time.

Of the sculptor mentioned in the succeeding
article I have lost sight for some time. He was
the author, I believe, of the equestrian statue of
the Prince Consort on the Holborn Viaduct.

"Mr. C. Bacon, a young sculptor of promise,
chiefly known by his statue of 'Mendelssohn,' the
inauguration of which at the Crystal Palace last
year will be remembered by many readers, has
lately completed a colossal statue of Sir John
Franklin. The result of a public subscription first
set on foot by the inhabitants of Spilsby, Lincoln-
shire (Sir John's birthplace), it is to be erected
on a granite pedestal in front of the Spilsby
Town-Hall. The casting of the statue, which is

of bronze, took place on Wednesday last at the
Grove Foundry, Southwark Bridge Road, under
the immediate superintendence of Mr. Rogers,
who for many years was foreman at the foundry
of Messrs. Cottam & Robinson, and until lately
directed the casting of all statues by that firm.
To Mr. Rogers is due the first introduction of
the system of casting large figures in one piece,
the practice formerly pursued by Chantrey, and
even still retained in many cases, being to cast
the work in three or more separate parts.

"Of the statue as a work of art it is scarcely
possible at present to form an accurate judgment.
The model from which the mould has been taken
was on view at the foundry, but huddled away in
a corner, and in a most unfavourable light. But,
as far as I could judge from that and a photograph of the figure, Mr. Bacon's statue promises to
be an honest, manly, and unaffected piece of work.
Sir John stands upright, leaning one hand on an
anchor, and grasping a telescope with the other.
The face is watchful and intelligent, and the sculptor, who made his first sketch under the immediate superintendence of Lady Franklin, has the
testimony of Mrs. Booth (the sister of Sir John),
Sir Roderick Murchison, Mr. John Barrow, and
many others, to the fidelity of the portraiture.
The details of dress and accoutrements are faith-

fully rendered, being free from any ·'high art'
idealisation, and the treatment of the whole figure
is broad and simple.

"Having paid tribute of praise to the sculptor's
work, I will describe as nearly as I can the scene
of Wednesday last.   On entering the foundry-
yard, the first object that presents itself is a tall,
cylindrical, rusty iron furnace, with a conical top,
through which sulphur-coloured flames and dense
masses of smoke are driving with fearful energy.
Within lies a boiling mass of bronze, the heat
from which is so great as to render the atmosphere
around most uncomfortably hot.   Passing through
an archway, we enter the foundry itself, finding
ourselves in a lofty, grimy, brick structure.   The
beams of the roof are black and discoloured, and
the windows obscured with dirt.   In the centre
of the compartment stands an enormous and
powerful crane ; boiler-plates, pipes, and all sorts
of shapeless pieces of iron lie about.   In front of
a round-headed aperture in the wall, which com-
municates with the furnace outside, is a trough,
inclining towards a large rectangular-shaped crucible ; in front of this, again, is an irregularly-
shaped ditch of about a foot in depth, the bottom
of which is perfectly even, and perforated with
numerous holes ; through these the metal runs
into the mould which lies underneath, invisible to

the spectator. Several long tubes stand up out of the earth; these are to allow the escape of the gases generated by the heat of the metal, which otherwise would probably burst the mould, or injure the work by air-bubbles. The ground on which we tread is composed of black loam and sand, of which also the mould is made. The process of making the mould is one of great nicety, requiring much time and care in its development, and as the least drop of water might cause the whole thing to blow up, the mould is carefully dried for many days. The preparations look so simple that one is almost disappointed. Forgetting that a bronze statue is in reality but a shell of metal little more than a quarter of an inch in thickness, a person unacquainted with casting expects to see arrangements on a larger and more imposing scale. That crucible looks ridiculously small, but it will hold about a ton and a half, which is more metal than is required for the casting of an eight-feet statue.

"As the time for the operation draws on, more visitors arrive; the place becomes gradually crowded, and the light dresses of the ladies seem to increase the dingy appearance of the building. The workmen complete their preparations; an iron brazier filled with burning coke, which stood on the crucible so as to dry and warm it thoroughly,

is removed, and every particle of dust or other
impurity in the trough, crucible, or entry to the
mould, is carefully swept away. Shavings are
inserted into the mouths of the air-tubes; these
will be lighted presently, so as to increase the
draught from beneath. The metal, which has been
boiling for some hours, is declared ready, and the
signal is given to begin. I thought of that amusing
braggart, Benvenuto Cellini, and his great excitement when casting his Perseus, how, when the
metal refused to run, he ordered all his pewter
dishes and porringers to be thrown into the furnace, to render it more fusible, and his noisy and
egotistical thanksgiving to Heaven when he found
the mould filling. There was no excitement here
—save amongst some of the visitors, perhaps—no
flurry or nervousness. Each man seemed to know
his proper duties, and performed them quietly and
thoroughly. At a French scene of this kind, we
can imagine that there would be much decoration
of the building with flags and flowers, and flourish
of trumpets, the inevitable soldier or *sergent-de-
ville*, and perhaps a laurel crown for the sculptor.
The quiet business-like air of the whole affair on
Wednesday was one of its great features. At a
very few minutes after the appointed hour, a simple
'Now then!' was uttered; and amid a silence,
only broken by the clank of hammers in other parts

of the building, a workman proceeded to let loose the stream of metal. Like a dazzling white thread at first, it gradually increased in size, and shooting forth little angry sparks, trickled down the trough into the crucible with a hissing, spattering noise, similar, only greater in volume, to that which is caused in the domestic operation of frying. The crucible gradually fills, the heat is intense, and the workmen protect themselves in some measure by interposing iron plates. The glare from the molten mass sheds a ruddy glow over each near object, and lights up the blackened timbers of the roof above. Some five or six men stand by with iron rods, which they dip into the scalding metal. The ends of them are turned instantly to white heat. Some whitish powder is thrown on and stirred into the glowing mass to facilitate its fusion, and at length it is suffered to run into the irregular ditch. Simultaneously the shavings in the air-tubes are set light to by the red-hot rods, and, as the metal finds its way down the holes, the gas rushes to the surface and burns in the tubes with violet and greenish flames. There is a sudden and violent puff, a gurgling noise, as the metal settles itself in every chink and cranny of the mould, and the interesting process of casting is over. It is pronounced complete and perfect : sculptor and founder are alike pleased, and the faces even of the work-

men testify that they have not been indifferent to the
success of the work. But something yet remains
to be done. The surplus metal, still brilliantly red,
and emitting great heat, must, ere it harden, be
detached from the 'runners'—the rods of bronze
which have filled the communicating holes. Accord-
ingly, all hands get to work, levelling the ditch with
the ground, and breaking off great cake-like pieces,
which are thrown on one side by means of shovels
or long pincers. There is nothing more to be
seen, for some time must elapse before the cast
is sufficiently cool to be disinterred from its sooty
grave. It is pleasant, after the heat and animation
of this scene, to emerge on the solitude of Southwark Bridge Road, and, after paying the misan-
thropical toll-keeper, who, cut off from the society
of his fellow-men, finds solace in the company of
a tame jackdaw, to stand on the bridge and breathe
the cool air from the river, which sparkles merrily
in the mild rays of an October sun."

I am tempted to give part of an article describing the production of a stained window here, partly
from my early association with "glass," partly
because I think the slight descriptive sketch would
be interesting to the reader. Some changes have
taken place, and I may have modified some of the
opinions therein expressed, but the statements
generally are as accurate now as when they were

written ; so without further preface let us visit one of the larger stained-glass establishments, and see how a coloured window is made.

" Here is the place : a tall narrow building with high gables, looking somewhat like a magnified Gothic dog-kennel. We enter the pointed doorway, and, passing through the office devoted to business details, come on a long, lofty, well-lighted room, the windows of which are broad and high, and furnished with apparatus for supporting those specimens of stained glass that are completed, and with black blinds for shutting off all unnecessary light. Around the walls are hung prints from the works of the early German and Italian artists, sketches made in competition for cathedral windows, a few plaster casts, rubbings of brasses, and a number of odd-shaped pieces of brown paper, that resemble somewhat tailors' patterns, but which are really the patterns of the heads of windows taken from the actual stonework, and sent here in order to ensure accuracy in the fitting of the glass to its stone frame. At an easel at one end of this room the master is at work on a drawing of the Crucifixion. His assistants and pupils are variously but busily employed. One is drawing heraldic lions and griffins of extreme tenuity ; another is occupied with the floriated or crocketed canopies and geometrical ornament which form the setting of the

figure subjects.   Boys with square and compass
are marking out the forms of 'lights,' on long
narrow strips of paper.   One of them, a very
small boy, is mounted on a pair of steps, drawing
a saint ten feet in height from one of the master's
designs.   All the cartoons are made here.   The
workers in this room give employment to the rest
of the establishment.   On each cartoon the shapes
and sizes of the various pieces of glass are marked
—the colours are indicated by means of numbers
which correspond with those on what is, with
pleasant disregard of accurate description, called
a 'pattern *card*,' a number of small squares of
glass (from 100 to 150) of different tints leaded
together.   The cartoon is next handed over to
the glazier, who, referring alternately to it and
the pattern-card, cuts each piece of glass of the
right size and shape.   The pieces having been
collected, are placed on a tray and sent to the
painting-room.   Here we find a number of men
seated opposite to the light, before easels formed
of large pieces of white glass and held in a
frame.   The design is copied on the glass by
simply laying the glass upon the drawing and
tracing the outlines seen through it.   The pieces
are next affixed, by means of small pieces of wax,
to the glass of the easel, and the flat transparent
shadows are then painted.   The glass-painter in

the mosaic method works with but two colours—
enamel brown and a yellow stain. The former is
a reddish-brown pigment, made either from iron
or copper. It is diluted with spirits of turpentine,
gum-water, or oil of spike lavender. With this
he marks in all shadows and black lines, or smears
it over the glass where diaper or other ornament
is intended to be placed, part of which, when
dry, is scraped off with a pointed stick, leaving
the diaper sharp and transparent. The painting
finished, the glass is next submitted to enormous
heat in kilns. When sufficiently baked, it is
suffered to cool gradually and anneal itself. There
remains nothing now but for the glazier to finish
the work. He arranges all the pieces in order
on a table, and surrounds each with a strip of
lead, somewhat in the form of the letter I viewed
sideways, the groove on each side receiving the
edges of the glass. Each joint in the lead-work
is carefully soldered. But rain and wind would find
their way even through the small spaces left between lead and glass, and therefore a cement is
rubbed in, which hardens by exposure to the atmosphere, and renders the window perfectly air-tight.
In order to obviate chances of breakage and unnecessary trouble in fixing the work in its ultimate
destination, the window is divided into convenient
portions, called 'glazing panels,' each of which is

surrounded by a strong lead about an inch in breadth. These are set up in the grooves of the stone-work and secured to the transverse iron bars of the window space. Packed in boxes, between layers of straw, the window we have seen completed is whirled by the goods train far away into the country, and fixed in its new home, where it will be the cause of much wonder and speculation among the humbler portion of the rustic congregation the following Sunday, or it may be destined for one of the 'City' churches, the gift, perhaps, of a wealthy stockbroker, who will invite his brother brokers to inspect it, and discuss with them, not its art, but its cost.

"Glass-painting was in its greatest perfection in the twelfth, thirteenth, and fourteenth centuries. In the florid compositions of the fifteenth and sixteenth centuries, the principles which guided the earlier and more simple-minded artist were neglected or forgotten. The Reformation was a heavy blow to the art, and little besides armorial bearings were executed in the reign of Elizabeth. What signs of returning animation were shown by it in the reigns of James and the first Charles, were speedily quelled by the rebellion, a period when the prejudices of men inclined them rather to break than to make stained windows. The taste for the art gradually died out, and few works to which the epithet 'good' could be applied were produced after the Restoration. The lustrous jewel-like look of early glass was replaced by heavy opaque colour, meretricious design, and disregard of constructive truth. The lead lines, which in the older styles, by following the outlines of the design, imparted strength to the construction and vigour to the drawing, were now looked on as unsightly objects, to be hidden when possible, and retained only through necessity. Thus white glass was chosen, covered with enamel surface colours, and cut into squares, giving a disagreeable idea of network. Towards the end of the eighteenth century, the west window of New College Chapel, Oxford, was executed by Jervis, after the designs of Sir Joshua Reynolds. Sir Joshua was utterly ignorant of the requirements and appliances of glass painting, and no wonder that the result was a failure, or that Horace Walpole should write sneeringly of 'Sir Joshua's washy virtues.'

"Glass-painting is beginning to recover from the torpor into which it had fallen, and to reassert its claim to be considered a fine art. It is yet much encumbered with the manufacturing spirit; the capitalist is at work as well as the artist. The same design is used more than once, and it is not uncommon for a set of figures which have already done duty as 'prophets,' to undergo slight modifications as to beard and emblems, and with changed

colours, to reappear as 'evangelists.' Still, as a
general rule, a better and more artistic spirit is at
work. In some cases the heads of glass-painting
firms are themselves artists, in others the best available talent is secured. The principles of material
and construction are now more thoroughly carried
out. A stained window should always look like
what it really is, a flat surface, and a vehicle for
the transmission of light. And therefore all rapid
perspectives, violent foreshortenings, and deceptive
effects of light and shade are inadmissible. The
composition and arrangement of the figures should
resemble that of a sculptured bas-relief, and no
more shadow should be introduced than is found
in the paintings of Giotto or Fra Angelico. A
certain heraldic outline treatment is necessary, and
all tricks of chiar'oscuro, such as the introduction
of lamplight in the modern Munich window at
Cambridge, are false and wrong, because, when
employed, all idea of flatness is lost, and they are,
moreover, inconsistent in darkening the illuminating
surface of the actual window, for the sake of the
childish trick of introducing a false light with its
own peculiar lights and shadows. But while
emulating the older windows as far as constructive
honesty is concerned, it would be well if a little
less servile imitation of the art of the past were
shown in design and drawing. The flat treatment

may be secured without having recourse to the
rigid attitudes, the splay feet, glove-stretcher hands,
and stringy beards of the Middle Ages. The old
subjects, too, are done over and over again with
but little variation in the method of their treatment,
and the monkish notion of Hell—a dragon-mouth

BIRDS, BACCY &   M^R H·S·MARKS AT HOME   BEVERAGES
WEDNESDAY, JAN^{RY} 21ST 1880
17 HAMILTON TERRACE. N.W
MORNING DRESS. = 8 to 12 p.m

vomiting forth flames—is repeated to this hour in
many a window. A little more respect for nature
and a little less trustful reliance on the conventions
of the past are needed by our glass-painters. The
old painters frequently represented the costumes of
their day. In the windows of Chartres Cathedral
are a series of medallions portraying artisans and

workmen of the thirteenth century in their ordinary
clothes, and pursuing their customary avocations.
The modern glass-painter is not equal to the task of
grappling with the realities of to-day ; but until he
can thoroughly sympathise with the world around
him, his art, however excellent it may be, technically
speaking, will in a spiritual sense be little better
than a ' rattling of dry bones.' "

CHAPTER XV

MEDAL DISTRIBUTION AT ROYAL ACADEMY

" THE 10th of December, the anniversary of the foundation of the Royal Academy, is a great day for the students, as on that occasion premiums are given to those who have best distinguished themselves in the different branches of study. The evening of Tuesday last was looked forward to with more than usual eagerness, as the present happens to be a 'gold medal year;' medals of silver are awarded annually, but the distribution of gold is a biennial affair. The gold medals, four in number, are offered by the Academy for the best historical picture, the best landscape, the best group in sculpture, and the best architectural design. Departing from its usual custom of selecting subjects for the figure-painters from Scripture or classic lore, the Academy, in this instance, allowed them to choose for themselves any scene of Shakespeare's "Merchant of Venice" for illustration. The Turner gold medal was offered for an English landscape; the sculptors had the remorse of Adam and Eve after eating the forbidden fruit (as described by Milton) allotted to them; while the architects were to furnish original designs for an Exchange. How many specimens were sent in I am unable to say, but only two in each class were hung on the walls. The well-worn incident of Shylock giving his keys to Jessica formed the subject of one of the figure-pictures, the other was devoted to the delineation of the Trial scene. The landscapes seemed to have been painted in a spirit of opposition, one being intensely hot, and the other as intensely cold in colour. In competition for the silver medals there were several half-length life-size paintings of a forlorn-looking female in a black dress, three of the whole nude figure on a smaller scale, a vast number of drawings and models from the life and the antique, and a solitary specimen of sciography, which called to mind the elaborate machine for drawing a cork invented by Hogarth's quack-doctor. To cover a tolerably large surface of paper with innumerable lines, and vanishing points for the sake of accurately showing the form of the shadows cast by a ladder or a railway-truck on an irregular surface, is a task which must require considerable patience when so much simpler means could be found, and the Academy do well to reward such excessive toil with a silver medal.

"The different works are hung in what is known as the Middle Room of the Academy, thus eclipsing for a time the diploma pictures which are placed there. Pictures and drawings are distinguished only by numbers, so as to avoid any suspicion of partiality on the part of the judges. There is a loud and busy hum of conversation and much gesticulation among the students as they discuss the merits of their brethren's work and speculate as to the result of the Council's decision. Naturally the pictures attract the greatest share of attention, and if two R.A.'s should stop for a moment in front of them, eager listeners press forward to hear any remark they may drop. The Shylock and Jessica canvas is evidently the favourite. It is painted with much facility and knowledge of pictorial effect. It strikes at the first glance ; the head of Jessica is true to the national type. Shylock and Launcelot are less successful, but there are brilliantly coloured draperies and numberless pleasant conventionalisms about the picture to atone for those deficiencies. Those who are not led away by a somewhat too

evident a tendency to picture-making, prefer its more
soberly coloured and, though more laboured, yet more
honestly painted rival, the Trial scene, a work by a
less practised hand, full of the crudities of conception
inseparable from the efforts of a beginner, but showing a fair conception of character and a determina-
tion to be as far as possible original.   After a time,
one of the porters, radiant in scarlet gown and
silk stockings, summons the students to the room
appropriated to the delivery of the prizes.   This is
the large, or East Room, but how different is its
appearance now to that which it presents on the
first Monday in May.   No acres of brilliant colour
and gilding meet the eye, no smell of fresh paint
or varnish assails the sensitive nostril.   The boarded
walls are painted a dull red, suspended on their
surfaces are one or two copies of Raphael's cartoons,
Rubens's 'Descent from the Cross' and Da Vinci's
'Last Supper.'   The room is longitudinally divided
into two compartments by a wooden barrier.   The
floor of the lesser is covered with red baize ; on
a raised daïs, extending the whole length of the
room, are placed two rows of chairs, that in the
front for the Academicians, that in the rear for the
Associates.   In the centre of all, there is a table
covered with crimson velvet, and a gilded chair for
the President : the whole forming a very imposing
and stately background for the ensuing ceremony.

On the other side of the barrier plain wooden
benches are fixed at gradually ascending heights,
and these are nearly filled with students and pro-
bationers, who seek to wile away the tedium of the
interval which must elapse before the arrival of
the President and the members by strenuous en-
deavours to turn the place into a bear-garden.
Pellets of bread and modelling-clay are thrown
about, zoological imitations, more or less successful,
are attempted ; some ingenious youth has brought
down a cheap mouth-organ, with which he emits
sounds such as those which a cow in the last stage
of consumption might be expected to utter ; nor
is that method of whistling through the fingers,
so successfully practised by the 'gods' of a trans-
pontine theatre, altogether unheard. These and
other playful tricks are accompanied by an incessant
stamping of feet and clattering of walking-sticks
and umbrellas. The red-gowned porter occasionally
opens a door a few inches and makes remonstrative
signs, but without effect, and when he enters for
the purpose of removing the centre panel of the
barrier so as to allow the medallists a free passage
to the presidential chair, the applause with which
he is greeted is something tremendous. On one of
the benches I observed four female students (the
Academy has lately opened its doors to the fair
sex), who crouched together, looking rather scared

by their first introduction to the humours of a 'gold
medal night,' and who must have retired from
the scene with splitting headaches. And now the
folding-doors are thrown open, and in march the
R.A.'s and Associates, headed by Sir Charles Eastlake in plain evening dress and wearing the Presidential chain and badge. Loud and long applause
greets their entry, followed by a breathless silence,
when, after all are duly seated, the President pro-
ceeds to make a few prefatory remarks on the
character of the works submitted, and congratulates
the students on the general advancement they have
made. In two cases, he said, honours would not
be awarded, neither of the landscapes being considered worthy of the Turner medal, and the paintings from the nude figure fell short of the average.
Then in clear tones and measured style, Sir Charles
proceeded to enumerate the successful candidates.
Every ear was on the stretch, and it was not difficult from nervous trembling of the hands and facial
twitchings to discover some who had been playing
for the stake. 'In historical painting, the gold
medal, the discourses of Reynolds, and other books,
have been awarded to Mr. Andrew Brown Donaldson.' The Trial scene, then, is successful after
all, and as its painter (a son, I believe, of Professor
Donaldson, the architect) emerges from the crowd
and passes up to receive the prize, given with

a kindly smile from the President, a storm of applause bursts forth from the excited students. Mr. George Slater obtains the gold medal for the best historical group in sculpture, and Mr. T. H. Watson for the best architectural design. The same ceremony is repeated some dozen times, and the decisions of the Council, judging from the enthusiastic demonstrations that accompany each announcement, give universal satisfaction. The list of prizes being gone through, the President lingers as if, according to custom, he were about to deliver a short address, but excuses himself on the ground of previous ill-health and his numerous and pressing duties, and so, with a few brief words of encouragement and incentive to the excitable audience, the proceedings terminate."

The above is an accurate description, written at the time, of the "gold medal night" of December 10, 1861. I give it in its entirety, for it may be said, from its age, to have acquired a halo of antiquity, and to possess a certain historical interest.

It will be understood that the scene is at Trafalgar Square, in the comparatively small galleries then occupied by the Royal Academy. The number of works sent in competition was equally limited compared with that of years past. Each year that number increases, and requires not one, but several galleries for its display. The old

"Middle Room" was a moderate-sized apartment, and might have been placed in the present Gallery No. III. and yet leave ample space to spare ; but No. III. holds but a tithe of the competitive works which overflow gallery after gallery in an all but endless stream. The scarlet gown of the porter remains, though of a different fashion, but the "silk stockings" have disappeared, possibly for ever. The distribution of the medals now takes place in the spacious "lecture-room," and the plain wooden benches are a trifle more ornate ; otherwise the arrangements, the double row of chairs for members, the table, and the Presidential chair, are much the same as of yore. Not so with the behaviour of the students, in which there is a marked change for the better. I have alluded in another page to their demeanour while waiting for the entrance of the President and members ; the preceding extract gives more in detail and without exaggeration the noisy horseplay and rowdyism which characterised these evenings. The presence of woman—the reader will note the allusion to female students—has largely contributed to change or modify this. Then but recently admitted to the Academy schools, they could be counted by units. In time the number gradually increased to hundreds, till they formed an important contingent of the students ; and now, by their perseverance and enthusiasm, prove they can

frequently be successful competitors in the race for
honours with students of the opposite sex, while
their gentle presence and womanly influence are
powerful agents in refining the manners and behaviour of the rougher male creature.

AT THE GRAPHIC.   J. D. WATSON.

CONNOISSEURS AND ARTISTS AT THE GRAPHIC SOCIETY'S MEETING.

CHAPTER XVI

PICTURES

1861

WHILE carrying out the designs of Clayton & Bell in All Souls' Church, Halifax, Mr. or Colonel Akroyd, as he was called, took great interest in the work. He was a man of taste and culture, had travelled abroad, and knew all the Continental galleries. He expressed a wish to have a picture by me. My work was known to him, as "Dogberry's Charge to the Watch" was then hanging on the Academy walls, and had been purchased by my good friend, Mr. Mudie.

I had a subject in my mind which I was desirous of painting, for which I got some suggestions in watching the progress of building the church at Haley Hill. It was a young monk carving one of the gargoyles or water-spouts of a cathedral in

Sulphur-breasted Toucan

39

course of erection. Subject was everything in those days, and the painter nothing if not "literary." It was not till the autumn of 1860 that I began on the actual canvas, having first made several sketches and studies and a full-sized cartoon. When the picture was sufficiently forward, I sent a careful little sketch and full-sized tracing of it to Colonel Akroyd. He wrote a kind letter in return, enclosing a cheque for £50 as part payment (the price had not yet been settled), but not yet deciding whether he would take this or some other picture. Meanwhile my artist friends thought well of my work, and some went so far as to predict for it a success. Sending in day was approaching, and the picture was nearly finished, when I wrote to Colonel Akroyd to say how I would like him to see it before it was despatched to the Academy. He started from Halifax for this and other purposes which needed his presence in town, but had not got half way before he received a telegram announcing the death of a relative which compelled his return. Then he wrote telling me to send the picture with a price to the Academy, where he would see it on the private view. Encouraged by the advice and favourable opinions of my artist brethren, the price had risen by degrees from two to three hundred guineas, at which figure it was marked in the Academy Catalogue.

The story of how "The Franciscan Sculptor and
his Model" was sold I heard at the time from Mr.
William Agnew, the present head of the firm of
Thomas Agnew & Sons. As he and his father were
walking round the Exhibition immediately after
the doors opened for the private view, the latter
noticed my work, and after looking at it a moment,
said to his son, "Go and buy that picture." The
son went to the Octagon Room, where the priced
catalogue used to be kept, and presently returned
saying, "But the price is three hundred guineas!"
"Go and buy that picture," repeated the father.
Mr. William Agnew had no sooner completed the
purchase, than who should walk up but Colonel
Akroyd. "That's my picture," said he. "It's just
been sold, sir," says the attendant. Mr. Agnew,
overhearing this, went up to Colonel Akroyd, who,
after mutual explanation, became possessor of the
"Sculptor and his Model."

It was a gratification to me that this picture had
been bought before the Colonel saw it. It was a
proof to him that if a firm so eminent were willing
to give three hundred guineas for my work, I had
not been demanding an exorbitant price. That
such a price was considered a little "tall" or "stiff"
in 1861 for the work of a comparatively unknown
man, was evident from an article in the *Daily
Telegraph*, in which the writer, after many flattering

comments, concluded with these words : — "We understand that Mr. Marks has sold his picture for the very substantial sum of three hundred guineas."

I felt I had achieved a success ; not a very great one perhaps, but of sufficient magnitude to be very pleasing to me. I had now turned the corner, and brighter days seemed to be in store.

On the morning of the "opening day," during the two or three hours that were allowed to outsiders for "varnishing" or retouching (we left at eleven, and the public was admitted at noon), I went up to J. P. Knight, the secretary, who was flitting from room to room, wearing an old straw hat, in which he always appeared at such times, to ask him if he thought I might now venture to put my name or "inscribe" it as a candidate for the Associateship. "Certainly," he said, "but don't make the mistake they all do, of fancying you will be elected immediately." "Oh, I shall be quite content if I come in in ten years' time," I exclaimed ; and curiously enough, on the 26th day of January 1871, just ten years afterwards, I gained the coveted initials.

It was not until 1863 that the following rule disappeared from the opening page of the Royal Academy Catalogue :—"Exhibitors of this or last year, being artists by profession, viz., painters, sculptors, architects, or engravers, and not under twenty-four years of age, nor members of any other Society of Artists established in London, are eligible as Associates of the Royal Academy, and may become candidates by inscribing their names, or communicating by letter to the secretary during the month of May."

By many artists this was considered an obnoxious and degrading law, and some refused to conform to it. I expect I was deficient in "proper pride" and did not feel its irksomeness to any extent. The registrar's office with the book for inscribing names was at the bottom of a stone staircase of some dozen steps leading from the entrance-hall. I remember dodging and waiting about the top of these stairs till a favourable opportunity would occur, when none whom I knew were looking. A hasty dive was then taken to the regions below, and the name signed. Coming up to the surface again, I breathed more freely, and mingled with the throng with an air of unconscious innocence. But this rule has long since gone to the limbo of the past. A would-be candidate for many years has been proposed by one member and seconded by another, as at any club.

When making the round of calls which the newly elected one made, and still makes, on the Academicians, I asked Mr. Knight if he remembered the question I had asked him on the morning of that

opening day. He did not, but told me of a fact
that I had forgotten. " You asked me," said he, " if
you should take to caricature rather than to painting, and I advised that, though you might make
more money at caricature, it would be better in the
long run to fly at higher game."

Knight was the teacher of perspective. I went
through the course of lessons under his tutorship,
and, in common with all the students, liked him for
his bright, cheerful, kindly nature. He made friends
of us all, and was full of fun and joke. He called
me " Punch " once when I was drawing grotesque
figures on the margin of the paper on which I should
have been working out the problem of the evening.

In the Royal Academy Exhibition of 1873 I had
a picture called " The Ornithologist," an old gentleman, with the assistance of his servant, rearranging
his little collection of stuffed birds. The floor was
littered with the worst specimens of the taxidermist's
art that I could procure. On a table in the foreground was a stand with some brilliantly coloured
examples covered with a glass shade, which, with
the ornithological properties, were supplied me, " for
a consideration," by a naturalist, as he loves to be
called, who still lives to witch the world with his
craftsmanship, and to whom I still go for skins, skulls,
&c. He expressed a wish to see the picture, so I

asked him to call some Sunday morning when taking his rambles. He came, looked, but said nothing. I began pointing out parts that I thought would interest him. "There's your heron, stork, &c." Still silent, I thought the glass shade, which was, as I thought, rather realistic, might arouse enthusiasm. "What's that little white ticket at the top?" he asked, pointing to the high light caused by the reflection of the window; "has it been bought at auction?" I meekly explained. "Ah!" says he, "you ought to put lights down each side; that's the way they're always done in our catalogues!" This man, who had lived for forty years among glass shades, had never observed in them the reflection of his shop-window. When I called his attention to one, and pointed out the "white ticket" with the sky and opposite houses in it, he exclaimed, "God bless my soul! now, I never noticed that before." My friend humbled my vanity on another occasion. "St. Francis Preaching to the Birds" had been sold at Christie's recently for a sum far greater than I got for it—reaching four figures, in fact. In the elevation of my heart I mentioned this to the bird-stuffer. "God bless my soul! think of that, now. It might come up again to-morrow, and not fetch two hundred!"

In the Royal Academy of 1879 I exhibited a picture called "Old Friends." It represented two old Greenwich pensioners in a shipbreaker's yard gazing at some figure-heads of ships, in one of which they may have fought with the enemies of Old England in the days of their youth. The background was painted from the yard of Messrs. Castle at the foot of Vauxhall Bridge, and is an accurate representation of the aspect of the place at the time. When I wanted the actual old-fashioned pensioner's dress, I had considerable difficulty in getting it. In the early autumn of 1878, two friends and I, one of whom had acquaintances in the town, searched Greenwich all over without result. Neither coat nor cocked hat was obtainable. We heard, to my dismay, of those articles of dress being used for the decoration of Guys on the anniversaries of the "Gunpowder treason and plot," and of their being destroyed in the usual manner. All had vanished. It seemed but a short time since I remembered the cheery old pensioners sunning themselves in the sunshine on the benches of Greenwich Park, and persuading you to have a look at the views afforded by the grand reaches of the Thames through their telescopes. I only looked once through the telescope belonging to a veteran, and the landscape seemed so blurred and blotted, so vague and ill-defined, that it had all the appearance of the work of a promising impressionist. But all things, all beings, are the victims of change.

Greenwich Fair, where Richardson's Theatre was the great attraction, a tragedy and pantomime got through in a quarter of an hour, was abolished in 1857, and eight years later, in 1865, the old pensioners had to bid adieu to their quarters in the magnificent Hospital.

After this fruitless search, I did what I ought to have done at first, and went to the Langham—not the hotel, but to the Artists' Society in the chambers of the same name close by. Here I got the desired cocked hat and coat, and was enabled to finish my picture. It was sold to a gentleman then collecting some English pictures for the New South Wales National Gallery at Sydney, where it now is.

In the autumn of the same year I was on a visit to some friends at Lewes, who had told me the celebration of the anniversary of the 5th November was a sight I ought to witness. "The Gunpowder-plot anniversary," as it was called in handbills distributed through the town, was got up by the "Lewes Borough Bonfire Society." I never before saw so many fireworks let off in a given time, nor bonfires of such magnitude. Hundreds of men—the bill said a thousand—in costume more theatrical than authentic, each holding a lighted torch, and letting off squibs or crackers at will, marched through the principal streets of the town.

Many of the houses were boarded up to some height above the pavement, not from fear of violence, for there could not have been a more orderly crowd, but as protection against accidents by fire. After much marching and counter-marching, "the gorgeous and imposing procession, extending upwards of a mile in length" (I quote from the local bill), marched through the High Street to the principal bonfire, in which the effigies of Guy Fawkes, the Pope, and Mr. Parnell, "manufactured by an artist and stuffed with fireworks," were speedily consumed amid the shouts and hurrahs of the motley crowd, while the strains of the National Anthem played by the different bands brought the proceedings to a close.

In the afternoon of the next day my friends took me to the museum in Lewes Castle, an *omnium gatherum* of relics and antiquities, genuine and doubtful. I enjoyed the quiet of the sunny autumnal afternoon after the noise and glare of the night before. The custodian of the Castle was an old sailor, who had served in the navy in the time of the wooden walls of Old England, when ships were ships, not unmanageable steel boxes of machinery, and sailing and seamanship were more than a mere tradition.

I soon got into conversation with the old salt, and the talk about shipping led naturally to figure-heads. I described my picture in detail, when he thought one of the figure-heads must have been that of the ship in which he had served. I promised that on my return to town I would send him a photograph of the picture. This I did, and in a few days received from him the following letter :—

" LEWES CASTLE,
November 9, 1879.

" SIR,—I am much obliged for sending me the figure head of my old ship the <i>Edinburg</i>, Sir i am confident its her head the more i look at it the more i reconise it, she was built in 1812 and i believe she fell into the hands of the Ship broker to break her up in the Liberal Governments reign, (Childers to wit.)—I am Sir your humble servant

JAMES MORGAN.

" Sir i will have it framed and keep it in rememberance of you and the old Ship.   J. M."

My first Academy picture of birds only, without human interest, was a group of adjutant storks. One of them is addressing his brethren, who stand around in attitudes of profound thought and meditation. The scene is a barren, sandy spot with a range of low hills breaking the horizon. Beyond the principal group a belated adjutant, half flying, half running, hastens to join the meeting ; for in meetings of birds or of men, whether small or large, there is sure to

Muscle.
STUDY FOR A WATER-COLOUR DRAWING, IN THE POSSESSION
OF HENRY TATE, ESQ.

be one to whom the sense of punctuality is denied,

and is always late. " Convocation " was the title

Mind.
STUDY FOR A WATER-COLOUR DRAWING, IN THE POSSESSION
OF HENRY TATE, ESQ.

given to the picture; it was hung on the line in

Gallery No. III., and, with another called "Capital and Labour," is in the possession of T. Ismay, Esq., of Liverpool. In making studies of the birds, I went to the Museum of the Royal College of Surgeons to take measurements of the bones, their proportionate length, &c. When I had obtained what information I needed, I came away, and crossing Lincoln's Inn Fields, it struck me that the occupation in which I had been engaged would furnish a good subject for a picture. I made a sketch of it, and my election as R.A. occurring early in December 1878, resolved that I would make this the subject of my diploma picture. I lost no time, for here was a debt which, however pleasurable, was still a debt, and I wished to signify my sense of the honour my colleagues had conferred on me by paying it with all possible promptitude. To get a skeleton to paint from was the first thing to be done. It was impossible to borrow one of those belonging to the Museum, though the Conservator of the time, Professor now Sir William Flower, kindly offered to do all short of that, kindly offering to have a skeleton placed in a separate room, or anything else in reason. And here let me pay a passing tribute to the kindness and consideration, and readiness to impart their knowledge, which I have always experienced in men of science, whether in their public or private capacity. But it was

imperative to have the skeleton in my own room, for
many reasons into which it is needless to enter here.
The Professor recommended me to an osteological
artist in Camden Town, who readily appreciated the
circumstances of the case, and within a few days
supplied me with a fine specimen specially articu-
lated for me, to be kept for an indefinite period, at a
very moderate rate of hire.   To paint that skeleton
required considerable patience.   I was continually
"losing my place" in the intricate forms of the
vertebræ, and had constantly to count them to
verify the correctness of my representation.   But
all difficulties were conquered at length, and the
picture sent off to the Academy, with the title of
"Science is Measurement," a title only decided on
after much discussion with brother brushes and
scientists.   A letter accompanied the picture, hoping
the President and Council would deem it worthy
to be accepted as my diploma picture ; and after
the next Council meeting I received the official
acknowledgment, which ran thus :—

"ROYAL ACADEMY OF ARTS,
April 16, 1879.

"DEAR SIR,—The picture 'Science is Measurement,' offered by you as your diploma work, has
been submitted to the Council, and accepted.—
I am, &c., &c.   FRED. A. EATON *Sec.*

H. S. MARKS, ESQ., R.A. ELECT."

The picture was placed in the Diploma Gallery at the close of the Exhibition, where with its fellows it now is, and will, with them, I hope, remain, until that day when London shall have fallen to decay, and Macaulay's New Zealander sketch the ruins of the city from a broken arch of London Bridge.

I had one year at the Academy a little picture of two Puritan sweethearts discoursing by a riverside gate, to which I appended as title the well-known lines, as I fancied, from Shakespeare—

> "Journeys end in lovers' meetings,
> Every wise man's son doth know."

Judge how surprised I was during the month of May to read an article in an influential morning paper in which the writer, while briefly referring to the picture, reserved his strictures for the quotation, as thus: "We earnestly hope that this quotation, with which we candidly confess our unfamiliarity, is not by any famous poet, since, logically considered, it is little less than idiotic. Journeys do not necessarily end in the meeting of lovers, nor is 'every wise man's son' qualified to pronounce an opinion on that or upon any other subject, seeing that the majority of wise men's sons, from the time of Rehoboam downwards, have been fools."

Here was a chance too good to be missed by

other journals, and on the following day one replied :
" Perhaps the quotation is little less than idiotic.
Only it happens to be by William Shakespeare, late
of Stratford-on-Avon, who wrote an obscure play
called ' Twelfth Night,' in which (Act ii. Scene 3)
the passage is to be found."

Imagine the glee with which critic No. 2 must
have chuckled as he penned this paragraph on the
slip made by critic No. 1, feeling he "had him on
toast"!   It is not entirely displeasing to a painter
to see the critics fall foul of one another.   A
second Shakespearian picture I had in the same
Exhibition, critic No. 1 was "down" upon, but
spared the quotation.   "We must needs return to
Mr. Marks, who invites the most careful attention
in ' The Apothecary.'   Here the sixteen lines
extracted from the world-famous description given
in ' Romeo and Juliet ' are of much value, as showing how completely the painter has failed in com-
prehending his author, or how deliberately he has
chosen to order his picture in direct contrariety to
the lines laid down by the dramatist.   Mr. Marks'
apothecary is not clad in tattered weeds ; his—the
druggist's—brow is not overwhelming ; his looks are
not meagre ; sharp misery has not worn him to the
bone ; he does not look like a caitiff wretch ; and he
is not ' culling of simples,' but is mixing of potions.
' Simples,' Mr. Marks, are medicinal herbs, so you

will find if you look into Dr. Garth's 'Dispensary,'
and to 'cull' means to gather, to choose, or to select,
and not to pour, mix, or infuse." Just so! but my
idea was to represent the apothecary mixing the
fatal dram of poison which he afterwards sold
to Romeo, saying—

> " Put this in any liquid thing you will,
>   And drink it off; and if you had the strength
>   Of twenty men, it would dispatch you straight."

His looks were as meagre and his form as lean as
I dared venture to make them without verging into
caricature. Farther on the critic objected, "We
cannot go so far with Mr. Marks as to admit the
appropriate presence in a mediæval apothecary's
shop of a human *radius* and *ulna*, with a skeleton
hand attached. An apothecary who kept human
remains, however high-dried, in his shop, would
have run considerable risk of being denounced and
arrested as a sorcerer." Here he was quite right,
and I can only plead, as Dr. Johnson did when a
lady asked him why he had defined in his dictionary
"pastern" as "the knee" of a horse—"ignorance,
madam, pure ignorance." "This picture becomes
the more exasperating when we consider the
splendid opportunity which Mr. Marks has missed.
From a Shakespearian point of view, the 'Apothecary' is a total and irremediable *fiasco*, but it will

possess rare and steadily increasing value as a mere painting, and as an example of bright but sober colour, and delicate but vigorous finish, worthy of the foremost Dutch masters." This little morsel of savoury jam concluded a somewhat lengthy article, and enabled me to swallow without grimace the powder of recondite learning which was its chief ingredient.

A PRELIMINARY STUDY FOR THE GREAT AUK'S EGG.

CHAPTER XVII

A PUGILIST PAINTER

I HAVE reserved this account of a professor of the arts of painting and prize-fighting to the last of these *Spectator* articles : it is certainly the most novel in subject, and for that reason more likely perhaps to interest the reader. Not every day does such a chance of good journalistic " copy " occur. Pugilists are plentiful as ever, but one who combines the art of interpreting the beauties of nature with that of destroying or damaging the form and features of a fellow-bruiser is not to be found every day ; and no great lapse of time intervened between seeing Mr. Ward's pictorial advertisements and going to see the works themselves to judge their merits. The ring has fallen into decay, the manly art of self-defence has become a mere money-grubbing pursuit, despite the fostering care of the sporting clubs and their habitués, who have spared no efforts in the attempt to elevate it into something noble and elevating! Science has given way to bounce and tall talk; biceps has conquered brain, and it will be long before another gladiator like the subject of this notice is seen in the land.

" Instances are not wanting to prove that the study of pugilism and a love of the arts are compatible. Byron affectionately refers to his 'old friend and corporeal pastor and master, John Jackson, Esq., professor of pugilism.' Many of us have read of Sir Thomas Lawrence's fistic encounters in Bristol Fields with the lad who afterwards became his model for 'Satan,' and the name of George Morland was often intimately connected with the prize-fighting fraternity. Mr. Ruskin considers that 'painting, as a mere physical exertion, requires the utmost strength of constitution and of heart,' and recommends the simultaneous study of 'all athletic exercises and all delicate arts.' The shortness of life is, unfortunately, inimical in most cases to the attainment of proficiency in both pursuits; the poet or painter may be but an indifferent pugilist, while the pugilist's attempt at painting would probably end in the production of a hopeless daub. His efforts at literary composition, judging from the advertisements in the sporting papers, are only remarkable for their manly defiance of grammatical rules. Nevertheless, at the present time, London boasts the possession of a man who has studied 'the art of self-defence' and the art of painting with equally happy results, of one who has taken the first pugilistic honours, and borne for some six or seven years the proud title of 'Champion of England'—though in the recognition of his artistic claims he has not been so fortunate: his name does not yet appear in the list of members of the Royal Academy.

"Of the antecedents of this remarkable man I am unable to say much. James Ward was born at Liverpool in 1801. His early life was one of hard work, being passed in ballast-heaving and coal-whipping. His pugilistic triumphs have been duly chronicled in *Bell's Life*. In 1832 he retired from the ring, and fifteen years later, being then forty-six years of age, began to practise painting, and has since continued to combine the somewhat antagonistic professions of a publican and an artist. I had heard rumours of Mr. Ward's pictorial bent, had occasionally come across advertisements which, with admirable modesty, announced the fact, that 'Jem Ward has just finished another picture which he will challenge the world for colour,' but never came across anybody who had seen a specimen of his talent. I determined, therefore, to go and judge for myself of the merits of this pugilist painter's work, and, contrary to expectation, found that it evinced much manipulative dexterity and considerable poetic feeling. If the pictures of Mr. Ward presented no points of interest beyond the fact of having been painted by an 'ex-champion,' a notice of them would have been out of place in the pages of this journal; but inasmuch as they really possess intrinsic merit, a wider popularity than they have hitherto attained may very fairly be accorded to them.

"In the far East, in the unsavoury locality known as the Whitechapel Road, stands a small public-house. A huge red lamp which hangs over the doorway proclaims it to be 'The King's Arms,' or more familiarly 'Jem Ward's.' Pushing aside the door, the 'host' is discovered standing behind the bar, dispensing beer and gin to customers whose apparel is not clean, and whose diction is strong. His appearance is not altogether refined, has more of the aspect of the ordinary prize-fighter. The head is broad, massive, and powerful, and the expression of the face honest, simple, and intelligent. Your errand stated, you are ushered by 'Jem' up an awkward staircase into a parlour of dingy aspect, smelling somewhat strongly of stale

tobacco-smoke. The low ceiling is blackened with
the fumes of the gas-jets. Around the room are
hung some eight or ten of the proprietor's *chef-
a'œuvres* in gilt frames, as fly-bitten as the walls
on which they hang. Other pictures in various
states of progress are stowed away in odd nooks,
their faces to the wall. A bench runs along one
side of the apartment, the furniture of which is
coarse and common, with the exception of a rose-
wood piano, the instrument belonging to the
painter's daughter, a pupil of Benedict's, and a
pianiste, I believe, of some celebrity. Such is the
studio of Jem Ward. A strange home for the arts
it is in the midst of the ceaseless roar of carts
and omnibuses, the continual cries of costermongers
and hawkers, and the frequent din of drunken
squabbles. Jem is his own showman, and con-
siderately saves his visitors the trouble of venturing
any remarks upon his pictures by criticising them
himself. Diffidence is evidently a word of the
meaning of which he is ignorant, and any tribute
of praise that may be awarded to his work is
accepted not as a compliment, but as a king accepts
the homage of a subject. In his own opinion,
few men, if any, have the advantage of him either
as a painter or a connoisseur. To quote his own
words, 'he can do all that Turner could in colour
and "atmosphere,"' which he considered his *forte,*

though he confesses that Turner surpassed him in 'detail.' That which has baffled the skill of so many painters, the imitation of the subtle hues of human flesh, is no mystery to Mr. Ward. *He* finds it 'very easy.' The old masters he considers almost unapproachable in this, but allows that Etty occasionally succeeded well.

" I had no opportunity of testing the accuracy of the ex-champion's opinions as to the facility he enjoyed in flesh-painting, no portraits or figure subjects by him being at that time in the house. A coarse-coloured lithograph, from a picture he painted of the fight between Sayers and Heenan, hangs in the bar; but this, of course, only gives an idea of the arrangement of the figures. The original was painted in opposition to the representation of the 'great event' published by Mr. Newbold, the cheap print-seller in the Strand. Jem Ward's version has at least this advantage over its rival, that the figures it contains are, for the most part, directing their gaze to the main business in hand, while in the Newbold print at least half the spectators are turning their backs on the contest, and testify utter indifference to its result by glaring out of the picture with most unprofessional concern. In other respects there is much similarity between these works, and both enforce the same moral with equal power. The coarse, degraded features of the 'fancy' multitude, represented in each specimen with harsh literality unredeemed by any refinement in art, afford a very strong argument in favour of the suppression of the prize-ring. Turner, to whom Mr. Ward so often compares himself, has evidently been the model on which he has formed his style. One picture, an English landscape with some sheep in the foreground and a brilliant sunset sky, resembles somewhat the style of Constable in the execution of the foliage. This is one of the most defined and finished works of the painter, but in general they all resemble more or less the later manner of Turner. Venetian scenes there are, with the sea and sky blending into each other in a suffused mass of light, revealing glimpses of hazy, pinky buildings, opposed by dark gondolas and vessels in the foreground. A cattle-piece, in which two cows are painted with a Morland-like power of brush, is so good, and the back of the canvas looks so old, as to raise in my mind the unamiable suspicion that it is some 'lot' purchased at a sale, and since invested with 'colour and atmosphere' by Jem. But be this as it may, I saw ample evidences of his artistic faculty. His pictures are painted with great solidity, firmness, and a reckless power of hand, such as one might expect from a practised bruiser. They display a strong appreciation of colour—not true colour, perhaps, in many cases, but often beautiful in itself—and though frequently strong and brilliant, in no one instance does it betray the slightest suspicion of *vulgarity*. ' Here,' said he, turning a picture from the wall, placing it in a favourable light, and rubbing his moistened hand over parts that had lost their richness—' here's colour if you like ; no one can beat that—it's soft and blooming like a peach. All done with the palette-knife. Here's a pair, now, just begun ; laid in the foundation, you may call it ; don't know what I shall do with 'em yet, no more than a baby. When an idea strikes me, I shall take 'em up and put in my detail. Some little cattle on the hills here, perhaps a figure or two, and there you are. I could knock off a couple of pair of them in a week if I'd only time, but when you're in business, you're always being called off—you lose your idea, and then you're done. Sunday morning's about the only time I can get to work. I sit down here with my colours on a large slab (don't use a palette), put my canvas on the back of that old chair, mix up the paint till I get a nice bit of colour, and then on it goes with the palette-knife. Never mix the colours much ; if you do you can't get richness or transparency : the fewer the colours the better.' In this last sentence it will be observed that Mr. Ward echoes, unconsciously perhaps, the precepts of the old Venetian masters.

" I have said that some of Jem's landscapes bear resemblance to Turner's later works. They would certainly deceive the superficial observer, and a tolerably near inspection would be required ere the practised eye could determine their author. It is not surprising, therefore, nor incredible, when the painter assures you that pictures he has given away, or sold as his own, have been vended by unscrupulous dealers as coming from the hand of the greatest landscape painter. Mr. Ward strongly insists on the stability of his work, from the simplicity of his materials and execution. Time, which injures and destroys other pictures, respects the works of Jem. It even improves them. 'I've been into places,' said he, 'where pictures of mine have been hanging; some I hadn't seen for a long time, and I couldn't believe my own eyes at first; they looked so much better than when I painted 'em. "God bless my soul!" I said, *they seem too good for me. They looked like old masters."' Though opinions may differ as to the estimate of Mr. Ward's pictorial capacity, I think few will deny, after inspection of his works, that he has somewhat of the 'immortal element.' Had his life been cast in a different lot, we might have had great things from him. Pictures far far below his standard may be seen by scores in any of our annual exhibitions. The painter's egotism is not surprising in one who has not measured his work with that of others ; moreover, it is an inoffensive and amusing egotism, while there is something almost touching in the thought of this sexagenarian gladiator snatching a brief solace from the noise and tumult of a public-house bar, and creeping to his little room above, there to paint with all the eagerness of a boy, and think of Turner and the 'old masters.' "

I will also make it a possession for the Bittern.

Isaiah

CHAPTER XVIII

ILLUSTRATED PAPERS AND ARTISTS' PICTURE SUNDAY

F ROM the middle of the month of March till the days when pictures are sent to the Royal Academy and elsewhere for the annual exhibitions, the artist has a bad time of it. Every creature has a parasite—the artist has several, and must endure the attacks of hundreds, among other delights of returning spring. The proprietors of journals, of which some are of established reputation, and others not yet known to fame, are now athirst for artistic news, and request information about the pictures you are painting, and to what Exhibition you intend to send them. Unlike the autograph-hunter, who apologises for taking up "your valuable time," these gentlemen think your time of no value whatever. Applications come from all parts of the kingdom. The task of answering each one would necessitate the services of a secretary, but the greater proportion find a facile route to the fire or the waste-paper basket. Other editors, less modest, ask for a drawing or sketch of your productions for his periodical, or at least a photograph, to be reproduced therein. Mr. H. Blackburn was the first to start an illustrated catalogue of contemporary pictures in this country, and has now a host of imitators. The first part of "Academy Notes" appeared in 1875, and was adorned by slight sketches, chiefly made by the artists themselves, of their pictures. These sketches were sufficient to recall to the memory the original works, without in any way competing with their interest. They were mere memoranda, and in no way facsimiles. As time went on, the sketches became gradually ousted, and were supplanted by photography. The imitators soon saw their opportunity—the game was amusing and remunerative, for the simple artist asked nothing for copyright. Journals and catalogues illustrated with reproductions by mechanical process increased and multiplied by the score, until matters got to such a pitch that in 1892 no less than three papers with several pages of illustrations of some of the principal works then hanging on the Academy walls were published *on the evening preceding the private view*, or *three days before the public was admitted to the Exhibition!* It must be evident that the interest of the Exhibition to the general public must have been considerably forestalled by this action.

But other ills arise from the wholesale reproduction of pictures during exhibition. A logical, well-written pamphlet appeared last year while the Academy was open, with the title "A Letter to Artists from an Artist." It bears no name of printer or publisher, and I have not been able to discover the author. It dwells on the consequences arisen, and likely to arise in greater strength and volume, under present conditions. Short as the pamphlet is, it is too long for me to quote at any length—I might be accused of the crime of padding—yet I cannot resist quoting a few gems of common sense.

" Few works of even the highest excellence are sold in an Exhibition after the first flush of novelty has passed away. It is only those well acquainted with the picture buying and selling world who thoroughly understand the difficulty of selling even a very attractive work in any Exhibition after the first few weeks have passed ; but how much is this difficulty augmented to-day, owing to the catalogues and illustrated papers, since the public, even those who have not visited the Exhibition, have already been confronted by so many reproductions of it, that as they open each new paper, they do not even care to examine what they already know so well.

" Why should a man give his hundreds for what in a fairly complete form A. and B. can buy for sixpence or a shilling, for what he sees spread out on railway station bookstalls, and sold in the streets outside the Exhibition, and repeated from the same plate in almost every illustrated paper ? "

" The publishers' theory of 'advertising' the artist and his works is not a very pleasant one for the artist to contemplate, though no doubt those who bring it forward do so in perfect good faith ; but it is necessary to expose its fallacy. The very first principle of advertisement surely must be to excite interest in any particular ware that the advertiser has for sale, so as to increase the demand for it. In the case of a new play, an opera, a book, a piece of music, or, in fact, anything except the work of the simple artist, great care is taken to excite this interest without in any way compromising the valuable quality of novelty. What would Mr. Gilbert or Sir Arthur Sullivan say if some enterprising editor were to ask them, on the eve of the production of an opera, to let him have proof of the music and the score, as he was anxious to print them in full in an early edition or 'a special supplement' of his paper? And yet he would be asking no more than the artist so easily grants. It is true that the colour and actual material is wanting, but so also would be the scenery, the singing, the acting, and the pretty faces and costumes. In point of fact, there would be more left out in the case of an opera than in that of a picture; but we all know that the editor's request would be received with shouts of laughter."

" In point of fact, it is well known that everything except a soap must, if advertised at all, be put forward in some different material or aspect to the thing itself. There is no danger in sending a small cake of soap; mere width of notoriety in the case of a soap may be of great use to the seller of it, and the sample sent cannot use up the demand; but the same kind of notoriety may be worthless to an artist, and will not enable him to sell his works. Every one wants soap, but very few want or can afford to buy a picture; and when they do, they want something that does not already belong to the world at large. To advertise a work of art, in the true sense of the word, is one thing; to make it common property by numberless reproductions is a very different matter."

" During the growth of the system there has been a steady decrease in the demand for and sale of works of art, and its present complete and almost universal adoption is accompanied by all-round depression in the sale of pictures of a character unknown in the profession for many years. Contemporary also with this system has been the continuous decline of the art of engraving, with which the question of copyright is so intimately connected."

The writer then suggests the following remedies for protecting the artist's interests :—

In the first place, to rigorously exclude the *facsimile* reproduction of his work from all illustrated catalogues, and return to the pen, pencil, or charcoal sketch, so excellent as a mere memorandum of his work, and in itself so absolutely safe.

In the next place, to meet with a steady refusal all requests to have his works reproduced by *facsimile* process in any illustrated periodical, or any publication whatever ; or if, after due consideration, he finds that he can afford to lend his work for that purpose, at least to prohibit its publication till *after the close of the Exhibitions.*

Some years before this pamphlet appeared I had written some verses touching briefly on the same grievance. Though printed only for private circulation, they found their way into one or two journals, and aroused ire and wrathful comments. In writing them, I can honestly say I was not actuated by any angry feelings.   It was the principle, not persons, I wished to satirise in these verses, which have in no way interfered with the friendly relations existing between Mr. Henry Blackburn and myself, for instance ; in proof of which I may mention that in "Academy Notes" for 1893 and '94 will be found slight sketches made by me of pictures I had in the Exhibition of those years.   Without further preface here are the verses :—

THE PAINTER'S PARASITE.

Scarce has the genial warmth of Spring
    Dark dreary Winter put to flight,
Than rousing from his torpid sleep,
    Awakes the Painter's Parasite.

What is he ?   Why, a journalist,
    One of that large and lusty band
Which preys upon the Artist folk,
    His *habitat* is in the Strand.

And every year he wants a sketch
    Of what you to the R.A. send,
Or failing that, a photograph
    Which he can reproduce and vend.

" Art Editor " he calls himself,
    Creature of cunning, more than thought ;
He knows the simple painter will ،
    Both time and drawing give for naught.

'Tis nearly now twelve months since he
  Attempted last to suck your brain,
And what you gave him gratis then
  He turned to most successful gain.

Ah! brothers all! if you'd combine
  To strike, as other workmen do,
You soon would from this farce be free,
  And quell the Parasitic crew—
    But you won't!

When we consider that artists as a body are the easiest going and best-natured of men, I am doubtful if "A Letter to Artists" will have any effect; nor am I vain enough to imagine for one moment that the verses quoted above will have any. In one respect, however, there has been some slight improvement. The artist is no longer expected to give the right of reproduction for nothing. In 1893 a new arrangement was carried into effect. An enterprising firm—I see no reason why I should withhold their name—Messrs. Cassell, made proposals to the artists that their firm should take the whole business of reproduction into their hands, paying a modest fee for the sole and entire privilege, and allowing permission to proprietors of illustrated journals and catalogues to publish copies by paying a small fee, which fees were eventually to be handed to the artists. Here, at the time when I write these lines (November 1893), the matter rests.

A form of parasite who is difficult to shun, for
his attacks are persistent and unwearying, is the
seeker of early information as to what pictures are
going to the different Spring Exhibitions. The
editors of some journals send round a printed
circular requesting a written description of your
work and the Exhibition for which it is destined.
But this is an old-fashioned method. The new
journalism is more hardy and adventurous. It
sends out its emissaries to invade your studio, and
effect the double purpose of a sight of your picture
and an interview with yourself. Should ingress be
obtained, you will not be surprised if in due time
you find a description of your work, generally in-
accurate, and minute details of your studio, its contents, and your personal peculiarities. For example,
some few years ago, I was finishing a picture for
the Academy. It was an open-air subject, and I
was painting in the "glass-house" portion of my
studio, wearing an old hat to protect my head from
the down draught which came from the skylight.
Presently there was a knock at the studio door, to
which there is an approach by the side of the house
for the convenience of models, frame-makers, &c.
Reluctantly leaving my work, I incautiously opened
the door, and seeing a smartly dressed lady, supposed her to be a model, for the ladies of that profession are frequently more gorgeously got up than

the wives or daughters of artists. "I'm not painting any ladies just now," I said; "will you leave your address?" "Oh! I'm not a model," replied she, bridling up; "I represent the *Toronto Twaddler*, and am writing a descriptive article of pictures going to the Academy." Apologising for my mistake, which was the more pardonable as the lady came by the back-way, I ventured to suggest that she had come early in the year—the month was February—when she brushed past me, and talking volubly the while, took mental notes of everything she saw. A short time afterwards I happened to see, not in an American journal, but in one of the evening luminaries of our native press, some highly interesting remarks about my work, studio, and personal appearance. Among other things, I learned "that the approach to my studio, which is not a 'show' one, is through the stables; that I have a florid complexion, grey hair and beard, *and always paint with my hat on!*"

To avoid similar interruptions during work by people who would obtain entrance to the house by any way rather than the legitimate one, known as the front door, I caused a small hinged grating to be inserted in the door of my studio, which opens on the garden. Through this little grille I can reconnoitre and parley with the besieging party, and grant or withhold permission to enter the castle.

A considerable fund of amusement may be found
in the pages of those newspapers addicted to gossip
on painting and other arts.   In the columns headed
" Art and Artists, " " Painters and Pictures, " and
similar titles, items of news of the most surprising
and marvellous character may often be discovered.
Not long ago I read that the Presidents of the
Royal Academy with but one exception have been
unmarried.   As the officers of a celebrated regi-
ment were said never to dance, so every President
of the Royal Academy has eschewed matrimony.
The accuracy of this statement is hardly borne out
by facts.   Of the seven Presidents who have worn
the chain of office—(may it be long before an eighth
is added to the list !)—no fewer than four have been
married.   There was a Lady West, a Lady Shee,
a Lady Eastlake, and a Lady Grant.   Again, I
read lately that a distinguished and well-known
artist had not been elected an A.R.A. because the
President had withheld his vote.   As the President
never votes except in cases where there are ties
either at the election of members or selection of
pictures, when he has the power of giving the
casting or decisive vote, this information is almost
comic in its inaccuracy.   Instances of similar want
of knowledge of most easily obtainable facts might
be multiplied *ad infinitum*.   When I see such errors
scattered broadcast over the columns of many of

the ordinary channels of information, I am often tempted to wonder if, in other matters of which I am more or less ignorant, the statements I read are in any way reliable. The acts, opinions, and complaints of great statesmen are described so differently by different journals, the proceedings of the collective wisdom of the nation—a wisdom not wholly un-mixed with rowdyism and some tendency to gar-rulousness—are shown from so many points of view that I am simply bewildered. How can I, in the face of such conflicting statements, arrive at a satis-factory conclusion? It is for this reason, and I say it with sincere regret, that up to the present I have been unable to formulate a political creed.

We are or should be never too old to learn. In some of the unconsciously humorous paragraphs of the Art columns I am told certain things about myself of which I was not aware. Thus, I did not know until I saw the announcement in print that I have "a singular fancy for collecting boots or shoes to which any historic value or interest is attached." I have "a rare collection of boots and shoes of the last two centuries." The fancy is "singular," no doubt—the more so as it exists only in the imaginative brain of the journalist. Another of my hobbies, I learn, is "that of col-lecting wigs." Who is the genius who invents these rumours? He has a brilliant fancy—I should

like to know him, to shake him warmly by the
hand.   I possess fewer wigs and shoes by far than
any painter who produces costume-pictures.

But the most astounding assertion follows, in
which I am told that I am "a singularly laborious
worker, and so devoted to my art that I can rarely
be induced to take a holiday from my easel!"
That I have done a fair share of hard work in my
time I admit, but that it is difficult to tear me from
the easel I utterly deny.   I venture to say, that
not one of my intimate friends would confirm such
an   unwarrantable   aspersion   on   my   character.
Regardless of Sir Joshua's dictum that an artist
should never be seen out of his painting-room in
daylight, I make a point of being out of it and in
the open air a certain portion of each day—as much
as I can, in fact.   I admit candidly that I am not
one of those enthusiasts who sacrifices his health to
his art.   I don't ever remember to have worked
from the rising to the setting of the sun, or to
have been found still brooding at my easel as the
evening shadows deepened and darkened around,
by a tearful wife and children imploring me to take
some necessary nourishment.   Bourgeois, Philistine,
soulless creature that I am, I never fail to hear or
be ready at the sound of "the tocsin of the soul—
the dinner-bell!"

My personal appearance has not escaped the

observation and comments of the newspaper scribe. I have been told that I might be taken for a sportsman, an assertion that does not altogether please me, for I regard sportsmen, with some few exceptions, with the same affectionate reverence that I have for a politician.

Again, I am told that from my ruddy complexion, and a form described politely as "portly," it might be thought I am a seafaring man. This is a compliment, for I have loved the sea—from the shore—and sailors all my life, but cannot think that I have any resemblance to those "that go down to the sea in ships, that do business in great waters." My appearance was, I think, more happily hit off by a friend, when, on my return from a lengthened stay in the country, he humorously inquired, "What is this mixture of the bold buccaneer with the captain of a penny steamboat?"

" The genial Academician " is a phrase continually connected with my name. Of my own geniality I am not able to judge, though able to judge that of others ; but I fancy that the street-boy who yells or whistles loudly as he walks beside me—the mate of the piano-organ-grinding fiend who asks for a copper—the model who comes an hour late and cannot even sit steadily through the effects of deep devotion to drink—and the begging impostor who by inadvertence on the part of the domestics some-

times, though rarely, gains admission to the house
and an interview with its owner—would hardly
employ the adjective "genial" as accurately descriptive of my manner. Of the word "humour-
ous," as applied to myself now for some forty years,
I am, I own, somewhat weary. In ordinary conversation I am often surprised that a remark uttered
without any thought of humour has been received
with laughter. Unlike other humourists, who are
allowed their sad or pathetic moods, I am always
mentally on the broad grin, or supposed to be.
Label a man in his youth, and the title will not
depart from him when he is old. In my art I
have never been—at least I hope not—didactic. I
am not conscious of ever experiencing the desire
to make men better in nature or loftier in aspira-
tion, and am certainly innocent of any wish, however faint, to elevate the masses. Still, when in
a serious mood, it is a little jarring to be told
that the results of that mood are replete with
humour of a dry if not racy kind. My work has
even been called "comic"—dreadful term! imply-
ing a depth of degradation and debasement seldom
reached by any except the lion-comique of the
music-hall. It is no use struggling against destiny.
Once a humourist always a humourist. The low
comedian cannot play Hamlet. But something too
much of this. Few men are interesting when

self is the topic. Let us at any rate change the
subject and glance at the humours of the painter's
" Sunday at Home."

"Picture" or "Show Sunday" has degenerated
from a simple friendly meeting to a crowded over-
grown abuse. In earlier times the painter invited a
few friends, who took some interest in him and his
art, to see what pictures he was going to send to
the Academy. The invitations included a dealer
or two, or such picture-buyers as the artist knew, a
race more numerous then than now. The invitations were not specially for Sunday, but spread
over the afternoons of a week or so before the departure of the pictures. By degrees Sunday asserted
itself and became the day, and pleasant gatherings
of private friends developed into hordes of people
one had never seen or heard of. Friends of your
friends sought admittance ; some came with intro-
ductions, many without. The shoals of visitors
increased yearly, few of whom took the slightest
interest in art. It became a fashion to do the round
of the studios, which furnished a topic of conversation among diners-out. From about two o'clock
until six on the Sunday afternoon, there is an
uninterrupted stream of callers. The street-door is
never shut. Carriage succeeds carriage. The street
is {blocked. Some art-enthusiasts come in their
own carriages, others in hired, others again in the

ordinary hansom, while a limited number employ the humble four-wheeler. There are two Show Sundays, one for the body of artists known as "outsiders," which is on the fifth Sunday preceding the Exhibition, and one for members of the Academy, which is on the fourth Sunday. Now, as it would be impossible to expect that the studio-haunter should remember these dates, the R.A. has to entertain two separate floods of callers. Between three and 5.30 the crowd is at its densest, and circulation becomes difficult. Some few show an interest in the pictures, and actually look at them, others stand with their backs towards them, while they talk among themselves on subjects that have no reference to painters or paintings. In such an assemblage the starer is sure to be present. He or she will glare around the studio at every object except the one they are supposed to come to see. Should the artist open his mouth to say a word or two in explanation of his work, the starer immediately fixes him with cold unglittering eye, never diverting it for a moment. It is evident that some of the starers find themselves in a studio for the first time. They glare on the modest retiring artist as if he were some recently captured wild animal of doubtful demeanour, to whom it is wise to give a wide berth, lest he should exhibit a tendency to bite or otherwise assault them. The

painting-room itself, the cage or den of the strange
creature, and all it contains, come in for a share
of wondering notice. "See," said a gentleman to
his pretty daughter, a girl of fourteen summers,
whose youthful mind he was imbuing with a love
of art, — "See, there is his engagement list."
"Here," pointing to a bowl of those implements
without which no studio is furnished,—"Here are
his pipes ; and look at that funny old gentleman,"
indicating a mask of Shakespeare, a cast from
the Stratford monument, in which I have failed
to discover anything of a comic nature. When a
visitor of a curious and inquisitive nature lifted up
pieces of hanging drapery to see what they concealed,
and turned the faces of different canvases to the
light which had modestly been turned to the wall,
I thought it time to venture a mild remonstrance.
There is always a man who, while calmly ignoring
your picture, asks if you have seen that wonderful
work by Mr. Malachite Green. Without waiting for
an answer, he launches into rapturous praise of it.
"Not only is Mr. Green's picture the best he has
ever done, it is a production of enormous talent,
a work of genius, and I have no hesitation in pre-
dicting that it will make an indelible mark, sir, not
only on the art of the country, but on the century
of which it is an emanation." During this diatribe,
so delicate in taste and tact, the artist feels low,

not to say humiliated. His picture, which he thought
"not so bad" in the earlier hours of the day, now
seems but a wretched daub, unworthy to decorate
the humblest wall. This pompous kind of oracle—
I am speaking of a type, not of an individual—must
be nearly allied to the individual so fond of writing
to the *Times* letters of a crushing nature, who never
reads for himself any item of intelligence that every
one else knows, but has "his attention drawn"
or "called to it;" who begins his second paragraph
with an emphatic "Now, sir," and ends his letter
with the remark, "Comment is needless;" after
which no more need be said. The oracle has opened
his lips, let no dog bark.

But I am forgetting the ladies, a great want of
politeness on my part, for they brighten by their
presence the place of the artist's labour. They find
an opportunity of displaying their fashionable attire,
for all are nicely dressed in harmonious colours,
though some of their garments may to the masculine
eye seem fearfully and wonderfully made. As a
rule, they don't look much at the pictures, a little
forgetfulness or indifference which may be the more
readily pardoned as they make ample atonement by
presenting to the now wearied eyes of the artist
forms and faces of beauty accompanied by the latest
and most charming triumphs of the milliner's art.
Now and then, but very rarely, a false note is

struck, as when a lady in a hat or cloak of exceptionally brilliant colour enters the room, when the effect of your low-toned picture is not materially enhanced by the contrast. The married ladies converse together—as where will they not?—on their children and their complaints. Great interest is taken in the latest state of Algernon's health, who has been suffering from measles, poor little dear!— and great the joy evinced when the fact is announced that darling Dorothy's whooping-cough has all but disappeared and she on the road to convalescence.

Before I had become seasoned to the chilling indifference with which so many people regard art in any shape (for we are not, never have been, and never shall be an artistic nation), I once ventured to suggest to a voluble lady, who had been gushing on all subjects but art, and was leaving the studio without having glanced at anything on the easels, that perhaps, as she had found her way to the painting-room, it might be as well if she looked at the pictures; but this was long ago, in the days when I expected too much of human nature. Another lady, who had left the studio of a landscape-painter in which two large landscapes were placed one at each end of the room, when asked which of the landscapes she liked best, promptly replied, "Oh, the *middle* one I thought the most lovely of the three!"

Such little ways are harmless and amusing by their eccentricity, but the studio-Sunday haunter has, I regret to say, been accused of offences that would seem to imply an inability to comprehend the laws of *meum* and *tuum*, or an utter disregard of them. Instances, happily rare, have been known of certain portable property disappearing from artists' houses and studios on Show Sundays—of that which is called kleptomania when performed by the rich and well dressed, and theft when performed by the poor and shabby. It is a well-known fact in the profession, if I may venture to use a term to which the music-hall artist considers he has an exclusive right, that one distinguished painter lost several articles of silver plate, and another some valued albums of photographs on one of such days. This was the reward for their generosity in keeping open house for an indiscriminate crowd of sight-seers. Wishing, as I do, to live at peace with all mankind, I would be the last to impeach the honesty of the humblest of my fellow-creatures; yet I cannot but regard it as a singular coincidence that the date of disappearance of some old-fashioned trinkets, such as seals and watch-keys, by which I set some store, and that of a particular Show-Sunday, should have been simultaneous.

The weather is proverbially fine on Show Sundays, fortunately. A wet day leaves unpleasant traces of umbrella drippings and muddy footprints along the house entrance, whether it be covered with the humble oil-cloth or kamptulicon of the old-fashioned house, or the more costly parquet, mosaic, or other expensive material of the modern mansion. As a rule, the weather is brilliant, almost too brilliant, with a cold blue sky, a hot sun, and penetrating east wind, which makes the office of speeding the parting guest, as he lingers for more last words near the street-door, somewhat hazardous. Show Sunday leaves several souvenirs at its departure with the members of the household and the maid-servants in the shape of colds, sore throats, and pulmonary affections.

I used at one time to like those Sundays. They signified the advent of spring—the season of perennial hope—that the labour and anxiety of the past few months would now give way to a brief but well-earned holiday. As they brought, by degrees, greater and greater crowds, and suggested problems of how to find space for an unknown quantity of people in a limited area, I ceased to care for them. I got tired of the humbug, of the hollowness, of the hypocrisy, they brought with them, and have now for some years discontinued the Sunday Showman business. I am told the custom is on the wane, but cannot speak with authority, as I have made but few inquiries, and held less conversation, with painters of my own age on the subject. I know, however, two or three friends who have thought with me, and abandoned the practice. Another reason for our giving up the Sunday Show was its entire inutility in a "business" point of view.

During a career of many years—a career so long that I never take up a newspaper during the art season without expecting to see myself affectionately referred to as "a veteran"—I have only on two occasions made a Sunday sale; and that was in the fine old time—will it ever return?—when pictures sold readily—when men who came to see remained to buy—when rival dealers vied with each other, as in a race, to be first at the desired goal, the studio of the fashionable or popular painter.

Some of the younger painters still believe in Picture Sunday. Those who work in a group of studios—a kind of artistic barracks—great numbers of which have sprung up of late years, club together and engage models to wait at the doors or conduct visitors to the different chambers, often a smart fellow disguised in evening dress, which sits awkwardly on him; more rarely a nigger or coloured gentleman got up with red fez, baggy breeches, and cummerbund, with yataghans and things. He makes a commanding-looking showman. When he talks, his speech has a suspicion of a Whitechapel

accent.   Young women habited in the neat livery
of the British parlour-maid make and serve out
tea, and its light accompaniments of cake, &c.
Luxurious chairs and divans, placed in the most
favourable position for viewing the pictures, invite
the guests to sit a while to recover from the fatigue
of looking at them.   In short, everything is done
to ensure the amusement, the comfort, and refresh-
ment of those who wish to kill an hour or two
of their Sunday afternoon.   Whether these attentions are rewarded by sales of pictures I am unable
to say.

H·STACY·MARKS
AT HOME
day Evening   189
17 HAMILTON TERRACE.
N.W.

PIPES, POULTRY, POTATIONS   8 TO 12.

CHAPTER XIX

LONDON

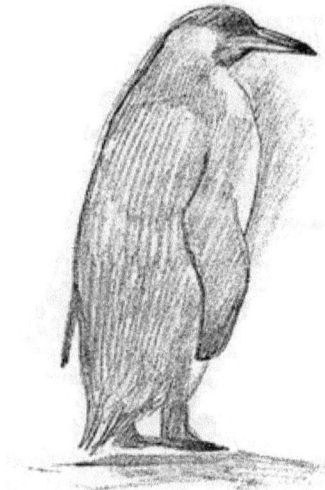

BORN and bred in London, and having lived in it the greater part of my life, I am a thorough Cockney. The more I live in it, the more do I like London. One of my friends years ago dubbed me "a police and pavement man." Another, with more ornate language, described me as "urban in my tendencies." Both were right. In common with Dr. Johnson, I regard London as the best place in summer—the only place in winter. Much as I enjoy a stay in the country sketching landscape, for I am no sportsman, I am never sorry when the day for return approaches. It is worth while to go away from town for the pleasurable sensation of coming

back to it. "Home-keeping youths have ever
homely wits," the reader may say. I will not
deny the soft impeachment. My wits *are* homely,
though I can no longer pretend to lay claim to
youth. I have never felt the desire "to survey
mankind from China to Peru," but am content to
study my fellows with interest and profit as I walk
along the London streets, or, when tired of walking, from the vantage-point of the knife-board or
garden-seat of a twopenny omnibus. Much may
be seen from the roof of a 'bus, with the additional
advantage of being in the open air. I say open
rather than fresh or sweet; for London, though the
healthiest, or one of the healthiest cities of the
world, has odours which are not altogether suggestive of "the perfumes of Arabia." A new wooden
pavement, with the hot sun shining on the asphalt,
stealing and giving odours, is not as pleasant to the
smell as a field of freshly mown hay. I nearly
always take my "carriage exercise" on the roof of
a 'bus when pleasure invites me to go by the way
which leads me to Hanover Square (the Arts
Club), or business requires my presence at extremely
rare intervals in the City, or to "the full tide of
human existence at Charing Cross." I am not "a
rat," the name given by 'bus drivers to the fre-
quenters of the Metropolitan Railway or "sewer."
Never do I travel by the Underground except on

compulsion. In a spirit of philosophical inquiry, I once made the experiment of a short journey in a third-class carriage full of workmen returning from their daily labour. The seats were fully occupied, and four or five men were standing between the rows of knees of those sitting down. The weather was mild, even warm, and as both windows were closed, and each occupant (all males) engaged in smoking some variety of villainous tobacco, the atmosphere was a little thick, not to say stifling, giving some faint idea of what the British soldiers suffered when crammed into the Black Hole of Calcutta.

The roof of a tramcar is in some respects superior to that of a 'bus ; the motion of the vehicle is smooth and regular, and free from the joltings so often experienced on a 'bus when the road is an old macadam one, and the 'bus not duly weighted with inside passengers. The fares are wonderfully low ; you may go to Greenwich for a few pence, and the passengers, if often of a humbler grade, are more amusing, and often more obliging, than those who ride in or on an omnibus. Now and then quaint scraps of conversation are heard from the garden-seat of the latter. I was coming from Kilburn towards the Marble Arch once, when we passed Alfred Gilbert's house and studio, then recently finished. The building is of the simplest possible

construction, being designed for use and convenience
rather than display. "What's that place?" inquired a passenger of the conductor. "Well, I've
been arst that question lots o' times. Some says it's
livery-stables—some says it's baths and wash-houses.
Blest if I know what it is." Coming to the
rescue, I explained it was the home and workshop
of the distinguished sculptor. "Oh, a sculptor's
studio, is it?" said the conductor. "Well that reminds
me that I see a little plaster cast being taken in there
one day." Another time I was edified by a very
young curate accompanied by two young ladies; he
spoke with a drawl that enhanced the brilliancy of
his conversation. "Is this the first time you've
been outside a 'bus?" he asked. This point being
settled, he further inquired, "Have you ever been
outside a 'bus at night? It's very jolly, don't
you know?—you see all the lights!" It is only a
few years ago that women first ventured to ride
on the roofs of omnibuses. They are accustomed
to it now, but for some time after the practice
was indulged in, the ascent, if made in company
with other females, was celebrated with considerable giggling, as if some very clever performance
had been accomplished. But the average young
man on the roof of a 'bus is my special delight; his
hardihood under the most trying climatic conditions
excites wonder and admiration. Having mounted

the 'bus in his usual idiotic fashion, carrying his
stick or umbrella with the brass ferule pointed
upwards, to the imminent risk of your eye, he
reverses his weapon, which he should have done at
first, seats himself, twitches up his trousers at the
knee, and should a fresh but mild south-west wind
be blowing, will pull his coat-collar well round his
neck, the waterproof apron over his knees, and
thus protected will be enabled to withstand the fury
of the raging gale for at least a mile and a half.
Languid from his great exertions in the City, he
will rest his feet on the seat before him, often to the
detriment of your coat-tails. Should a spot of rain
fall, he will immediately dive below to the inside,
either to protect his very shiny "topper" or to
prevent his virile body from catching cold.

I have hinted above that people are mostly as,
if not more, obliging on the tramcar than on the
'bus. I have often met with more civility from a
man in corduroys than from one who, by wearing
a tall hat and carrying (not wearing) a pair of
gloves of a prune-like appearance, thinks he may
possibly be mistaken for a gentleman. When I
have occasion to ride inside an omnibus, I find, as
a rule, the occupants are slow to oblige. You are
looked on as an intruder, and room made for you
leisurely and grudgingly. Ladies, I regret to have
to say it, are great offenders in this respect. While

expecting every politeness to be offered them, they give little or none in return. The conductor is often compelled to ask one of these immobile angels to "move up, please," to make room for the latest comer. They comply with this request more readily for a man than for one of their own sex. Ladies tell me that the rudeness of some of these females to other women is very marked. They will stare and glare at their victim or victims long and persistently—take a mental inventory of every feature, every article of attire or of ornament, and during the scrutiny coldly calculate the cost of the whole "get up."

The ignoble army of starers is of great and daily increasing magnitude. It includes members of both sexes and of every form of religious persuasion. Being of a mild, retiring nature, I have suffered much from the pertinacious gaze of the starer. The male starer can be coped with by fixing your eyes firmly on his boots (if you use an eyeglass all the better) and smiling never so faintly. This treatment utterly routs and demoralises him. Try it, ladies, the next time you are troubled with the bold gaze of an offensive male. It appals the stoutest starer—he can't stand it, but throws up the cards at once. With women-starers one has more mercy; you can't look at her feet unless you are an admirer of the enlarged toe-joints or bunions which they so carefully cultivate by wearing boots

with toes like V V's. The only remedy is to give
stare for stare, which, if resolutely done, is efficacious. Young women don't stare at the old fogey.
If they did, no doubt their gaze might be borne
with becoming resignation and fortitude by the aged
one. No, it is the corpulent, the elderly and un-
gainly, who glare fixedly at the youth of sixty
summers, who doesn't seem to care much for such
persistent attention.

On many of the 'buses belonging to the L. G.
O. C. there is a little printed legend which always
gives me pleasure to read. It runs to this effect:
"Dogs are not allowed in or on the Company's
omnibuses." This shows consideration on the part
of the directors for those who do not look on that
quadruped as "a boon and a blessing to men."

The noises of London increase with the growth
of the city and become more varied. The halfpenny press has been the means of adding a new
terror to existence. The average street-boy is bad
enough with his loud whistling, in which no trace
of an air can be discovered, and the awful yells, like
the war-whoop of savage tribes, which he utters as
signals to his pals to inform them of his whereabouts.
But he is a mild offender compared with the vendor
of the evening papers, who shrieks in your ear
"Extree speshal all the winner." It is easier for
the voice, though ungrammatical, to shout "winner"

rather than "winners" for any length of time, I presume—as a raucous-voiced lad told me in answer to my query, "Why do you shout Westmin-is-ter Gazette instead of Westminster?" "Well, guv'nor, I know it's wrong, but it's 'andier for your throat."

The extra specials give the very latest news on all matters connected with racing—not only the winners of to-day's races, but starting prices, latest betting, and other recondite details, which are Greek to the uninitiated. As the news-carts drive up from the offices of the journals and distribute quires of copies to the newsboys, what excitement there is among the beery crowd, what struggling and pushing and squeezing to secure the coveted rag which tells those who "have a bit on" of their own money, or of that which they have "borrowed" from their masters' tills, whether they have won or lost. Betting and the love of betting not on the increase! As well say smoking is not on the increase, when every street-boy has a cigarette which he chews and sucks as much as he smokes. There are large numbers of our fellow-creatures whose only literature consists of the sporting columns of the halfpenny press, yet the already heavily saddled ratepayer is asked to subscribe to parochial free libraries for the benefit of those who hate reading as much as they do work. Look at the pavement-loafer as he stands on the kerb-

stone of a crossing, to hinder as much as possible
the traffic of the busy pedestrians, if you care to see
humanity in one of its lowest forms. With hands
in his pockets and pipe in his mouth, he lays the
dust on the pavement by copious and continual ex-
pectoration. Does he ever work? Not if he can
help it—not, at least, until the bloated capitalist will
allow him thirty shillings a week for his labour,
and eight hours a day for his meals. He prefers
to let his "missus" slave for him, and by her hard
toil provide him with the great necessities of his
life, "beer and 'bacca."

The pavement-artist, or "scriever," as he is called
in the profession, holds the same position in the
painting world which the "busker" does in that
of music. The "busker" may be seen in front of
a public-house, generally on the cellar flap, playing
mournful airs on the cornet or violin. He is of
solitary habits, though he sometimes consorts with
a harpist. I have great respect for the pavement-
artist, and never fail to throw him a copper in
passing. "We know what we are, but know not
what we may be." It is not impossible, should
the great depression of trade continue, that we may
some day see painters of established reputation
chalking a mackerel on the pavement, and standing
by it in melancholy contemplation. When passing
by the brewery which stands at the junction of

Tottenham Court Road with New Oxford Street, few can have failed to notice a very youthful, nay, childish "scriever," a fair-haired boy of some ten or twelve years of age. I have watched him now for some years, whenever going that way, but in that time he has apparently neither grown older nor taller. He looks well fed, is neatly clothed, his face is washed. In better case than the average "scriever," he disdains the lowly pavement, and has an easel for his drawing, at which he works perched on a high office stool. A decent-looking woman, possibly his mother, attends on the boy, and at frequent intervals collects the coppers from the admiring crowd. There is little variety in the boy's art ; like many an older hand, he repeats himself, nor does his art improve. His subject is always the same. An attenuated lighthouse on the left, as white as it can be made, a vast expanse of very blue sea, and with still bluer sky mottled with pink clouds, which fail to impart any of their warmth to the ghastly white of the lighthouse ; these with a few ships or boats of original build are the main features of the design, seldom varied. In describing the quality of this poor child's work, I cannot do better than borrow a favourite phrase from a well-known art critic, and say that it "lacks tonality."

I was once going along the Marylebone Road, when I became aware of a "scriever" whose work

on the flags was of an order so superior to what
one generally expects to find in such a position, that
I stopped to look at it.   Landscapes and sea-pieces,
with effects of sunlight and cloud, and passages of
very creditable colour inclined me to think that
possibly the artist had at one time been employed
in some humble capacity in the scene-painting room
of a theatre.   With this notion in my head, I
proceeded to question him.   He at once sat on me
and shut me up by saying, " Bless your heart,
sir, I couldn't teach you how to do it,—it's a
gift!"   Then the curious loafers began to crowd
around to listen.   Our conversation was stopped,
and I compelled to retreat.

Sir John Millais once told me a good story of
a "scriever" who had operated on the pavement
of Palace Gate, at some little distance from his
house.   There were the slices of salmon and of
streaky bacon, the mackerel, the red herring, and
the broken plate.   These surrounded a head intended evidently for the Saviour.   Above all was
a hand pointing in the direction of Sir John's home,
with the inscription—"There lives the rich artist,
here lies the poor one!"

As I have girded here and elsewhere at the music-
hall and the so-called "talent" to be found within
its walls, I determined lately to go one evening and
judge if the entertainment offered to the public at

these now gorgeous palaces was above the average
of what I remember years ago when I visited more
humble Caves of Harmony. The first place of
the kind I ever entered was "The Malt Shovel,"
at Halifax, when I was staying there in 1859,—a
long, plain undecorated room, sufficiently lofty for a
gallery round three of its walls. It was sufficiently
dingy, and the orchestra neither numerous nor
select. The songs and recitations were stupid and
vulgar,—idiotic, but not indecent. It was here that
I heard for the first time the song of "Limerick
Races"—the only item in the bill of fare that I can
recall to mind. The next music-hall I went to was
the old "Oxford," then not long opened, and afterwards paid a visit to the "Raglan" (now possibly
extinct), and subsequently to the "Met," where I
had the privilege of seeing "the great Vance" and
"Jolly Nash." Some time passed before I again
entered the portals of a music-hall, and the glories
of the "Alhambra," the "Pav," the "Tiv," and the
"Troc" were to me unknown. One evening in
the early autumn of last year I broke through my
usual habit of staying quietly at home, and went to
one, at my own cost, the name of which I withhold,
lest guileless people should think I was giving
an advertisement. Arriving a little after seven, I
found a great crowd of people seeking entrance.
On going in, I found the three-shilling stalls were

occupied within a very short distance of a modest-sized pit. The five-shilling stalls, of which there were a considerable number, of course in close proximity to the stage, I was told, had been all booked that very morning. So far as I could see, what in a theatre is called the dress circle and the gallery were full. One or two private boxes had occupants, and very soon after the show began all the side-passages were filled with standing spectators. "Good business," indeed! No wonder that the theatres suffer if all "halls" are crammed like this.

It was not only in a spirit of observation and inquiry that I went here. My primary motive was to see Albert Chevalier, who has infused a certain poetry into the costermonger, and idealised him without o'erstepping the modesty of nature. I had heard so much of him from friends whose judgment I respect, that I wished greatly to see him and form my own opinion. I found, at the conclusion of the evening, that all they had said of his merits was not exaggerated. Mr. Chevalier sang three songs, "The Lullaby," "My Old Dutch," and "'Appy 'Ampstead." A scene was set for the first two songs, his performance in which, for there was as much acting as singing, was almost the only one in the whole evening that could lay any claim to art. It was true to nature, simple and manly in pathos. Both his Lullaby and the "Old Dutch" were rendered with an unexaggerated tenderness, so touching, that the sight of at least one of the spectators was dimmed by tears. I should be inclined to place this performance on the same level as some of Robson's passages in " The Porter's Knot," and I don't know how I could express higher praise. After this, with the exception of the Brothers Griffiths, true artists in their way, there was little one could commend. Their act, or turn, of "the lion and the lion-tamer " is a delightful piece of honest, mirth-provoking drollery, as good—it could not be better—than the " Blondin Donkey " of years ago.

Wherever else improvement may be found in the quality of the fare provided for an entertainment-consuming public, it must not be looked for in the music-hall. The same idiotic vulgarity, buffoonery doing duty for humour, and jokes of antediluvian feebleness, which have long since lost what little point they ever possessed, are as rapturously received as ever. Drunkenness and questionable midnight adventures are still the stock themes : a voice utterly destitute of any musical quality, a red nose, and ridiculous absurdity of costume, trousers too short, or a coat split up the back, are the chief requisites of the stock-in-trade of the music-hall " Comedian." Heaven save the mark ! But a more ghastly figure than the " Comedian " is the " Comedienne " or Serio-comic lady. What subtle distinction there is between the two I am unable to perceive.   Both mistake effrontery for archness, and appear to think that the more they can unsex themselves, and efface every quality of that womanhood which old-fashioned people are still prone to believe in and respect, the more applause will they obtain from the crowd of not too intelligent admirers. " How can I sing when you're winkin' at me?" chants one young lady as she looks at some noodle in the audience.   Another flirts with members of the orchestra, calls attention to the nose of this, to the eyes of another, receives a rose from the leader of the band, and kisses her hand to him in return. It is possible the musicians may not feel flattered by these delicate but rather too public attentions, in which case I hope their endurance is considered when pay-day comes round.   What becomes of the serio-comic lady when, of a certain age, she loses her good looks?   She has little else to recommend her, judging from the specimens I saw ; her dancing or singing is but second or third rate. Her strong points are unbashful sauciness and a certain theatrical prettiness.   Let us hope she gets married to one of that large section of the superior sex which becomes infatuated to madness with the woman who exhibits herself for a shilling.

In the half-dozen books of Familiar Quotations I possess, I have searched in vain—possibly because

it is a familiar quotation—for the author of "Give
me the making of a nation's songs, and I care not
who makes the laws."* Gracious powers! Let
me quote the chorus of a song sung by a serio-
comic lady, to the delight of the youth of the day.
After reading it, I don't think I can be accused of
over-estimating the depths of drivelling imbecility
to which the music-hall stage has sunk.

> "G'arn away! do yer take me for a silly?
> G'arn away! do yer take me for a J?
> Yer think yer've got me for a mug—well I'm sure!
> Strike me up a mulberry, what d'yer take me for?
>   Eh! what d'yer take me for?"

Shades of Shakespeare and Suckling, of Burns
and Dibdin, protect us! Human nature has always
been the same, and in the time of these great ones
many rubbishy songs must have been written and
sung. Happily the refuse has passed away, the
dross destroyed, while the true metal remains. So
may it be in the future. May the lyrics of Tennyson
remain to future generations when " You can't judge
a man by his overcoat," " Daddy won't buy me a
bow-wow," and all songs of similar character are
consigned to the limbo of oblivion.

* Since the above was written I have unearthed the quotation,
which is in a letter from Andrew Fletcher of Saltoun to the Marquis
of Montrose, and runs as follows—"I knew a very wise man that
believed that, if a man were permitted to make all the ballads, he
need not care who should make the laws of a nation.'

But enough of the music-hall.   I have related in
a former chapter my first theatrical experience.
Pleased as I had been with the performance at
the Royal Pill-Box, I soon hungered after a more
satisfactory kind of theatrical pabulum.   Macready
was then playing a round of Shakespearian characters
at the Princess's Theatre, under the management of
Maddox.   I asked permission of my father to go
and see the great actor.   He readily assented,
feeling perhaps that I should go in any case,—
whether he granted or refused my petition,—and
one evening shortly afterwards, in company with
my old school-fellow before mentioned, was sitting
in the front row of the dress circle, having saved up
my pocket-money for the purpose.   The play was
" Macbeth."   Impatiently I listened to the strains of
the band, but the supreme moment came at last,
and up went the green baize curtain, discovering
the three witches.   From that instant until the end
of the performance, I sat as one entranced, and
eagerly drank in every word.   Macready of course
played the principal character ; Cooper, Macduff,
and I think the part of Banquo was intrusted to
Howe.   As I already knew the play nearly by heart,
I was the more enabled to enjoy it thoroughly and
follow every point.   I see Macready now, and recall
his actions and attitudes.   I dreamt of him at night,
and walked and talked in his manner for days after-

wards. What an abiding impression that evening
made on me—an impression which many admirable
performances seen since those early days have
failed to subdue or eradicate. I saw Macready
play several Shakespearian parts afterwards, and
some of his farewell performances at the Haymarket Theatre. "Lear" I specially remember,
with Miss Reynolds as Cordelia, and Mrs. German
Reed, then Miss P. Horton, as the Fool. Sadler's
Wells was a favourite resort of mine, where I saw
Phelps as Hamlet, Timon of Athens, Bottom the
Weaver, Bailie Nicol Jarvie, and Sir Pertinax
Macsycophant. I regret that I never saw his
performance when he doubled the parts of Shallow
and Henry IV. Rather dry in manner, he was,
though not a genius, an actor of great talent and
wide experience. A play at his house was a treat ;
so carefully did he train each actor and actress in their
parts, that the result was an *ensemble* of considerable
merit, and a pleasant contrast to the system of one
" star " supported by several " sticks." The actors
under his management knew how to declaim blank
verse with feeling for its cadence and rhythm, which
I fail to find frequently in these days. Charles
Kean was another good elocutionist, though ham-
pered by a most unfortunate voice. I was present at
his opening night of the Princess's, when " Twelfth
Night " was played, in which Harley the ever-

restless was the clown. I saw Kean in " Hamlet,"
Ford in " The Merry Wives," Wolsey, Sardanapalus,
&c., &c. I may here mention that the Hamlet which
pleased me most was that of Charles Fechter, who
rightly played the Danish Prince as a fair man with
flaxen wig, in place of the raven ringlets usually
associated with the character. With the exception
of the Frenchman, the actors above mentioned,
and others I could name, spoke the language with
clear distinctness. You might give a foreigner
a good lesson in the enunciation of the English
tongue at many a theatre some years ago, but it
would be difficult to decide to what temple of the
drama you would now conduct him with a similar
view. Notwithstanding Hamlet's much - quoted
advice to the actors, written more than two hundred
years ago, we have still many players who "mouth"
their lines, and have not "the accent of Christians."
In my Paris days, I went as often as I could to the
Comedie Française, where the language was spoken
to perfection, and in this sense I had a "lesson" at
the theatre; though I do not, in spite of modern
authority, regard it as a school so much, but as a
place where one may be amused and forget for a
while the worries of life.

I once went with my father and an old friend of
his, a great playgoer, to see "As You Like It" at
Drury Lane. There were no stalls in those days;

we sat in the middle of the second row of the pit, the playgoer's special part of the house, the best for seeing and hearing. I only remember that Mrs. Fitzwilliam was Rosalind on the occasion. As we came away, my father and his friend talked of their earlier theatrical experiences. The elder Kean was mentioned, and they told me how, when he was enacting Othello, whole rows of spectators in the pit would rise from their seats, and, with wide-opened eyes and parted lips, gaze horror-stricken at the actor during the smothering scene. Such a sight I have never seen in my time. Were the people of that day simpler and more emotional, or was the acting of a better quality than now? It cannot be that the audience was less intelligent than those of to-day, for it would be difficult to discover any plummet capable of gauging the low intellectual level of the average music-hall frequenter.

Apart from the legitimate drama, I have many pleasant memories of Lyceum burlesques, gracefully and wittily written by Planché, admirably arranged and mounted by Madame Vestris, as admirably acted by the inimitable Charles Matthews, Mr. and Mrs. Frank Matthews, with Miss Julia St. George as the princely hero. Who can forget those brilliant triumphs of the scenic art which made such a dazzling, sparkling termination of those pleasant Christmas pieces? Of Robson, great genius in a little body, as Shylock, the Yellow Dwarf, Medea,

THE SEVEN AGES.

CALVERT
MEMORIAL
PERFORMANCE.
THEATRE ROYAL
MANCHESTER.
OCT? 1ST & 2ND
1879

TOUCHSTONE AUDREY AND WILLIAM.

Desmarets, Daddy Hardacre in "The Porter's Knot,"
in which his pathos was so true and touching as

to beguile us of our tears. Of Alfred Wigan, the
accomplished actor of old Frenchmen, in the " Lucky
Friday " and the " First Night." Of the perfectly
presented pieces of the Robertsonian drama at my
first theatre, but unrecognisable under the thorough
and artistic management of the Bancrofts. Of the
sarcastic, witty, and refined operas at the Savoy,
where the female actresses and dancers can be
elegant, graceful, and amusing without depend-
ing on the exhibition of their physical charms
for success. As these and many other theatric
retrospections come crowding through my brain—
when I remember what enjoyment it was and is to
me to see a good play well acted—when I think
that I had a turn for reciting and song singing, I
sometimes wonder that I did not become an actor.
Had an opportunity offered at one time, I should
certainly have gone on the stage.

CHAPTER XX

MODELS

A CHAPTER may well be devoted to the humours and eccentricities of models. Mr. Weedon Grossmith has very cleverly rendered some of the characteristics of the model of to-day in his amusing piece " The Commission," and the part is as admirably acted by Mr. Brandon Thomas. I have had many models in my time, chiefly of the male genus. They are generally vain, and are firmly convinced that the artist owes much of the success of his picture

to the fact of their having sat to him, and assert
at least their equality to him by speaking of him
by his surname only. The model will, in some
cases, eke out the gains he makes by "setting"
in the day by becoming a "super" at some theatre
by night. There was one named Butler who was
the priest in the "Colleen Bawn" at the Princess's
Theatre under Boucicault, and a capital priest he
looked. Fortunately he had no word to say, for
his speech might have betrayed him. He was one
of the old-fashioned kind, more respectful than
those of to-day, would give the prefix of "Mr."
to an artist's name and address one as "Sir." His
memory was very defective, to an extent which was
almost comic. Thus he would say, "I was a settin
to a gentleman named——Dear me! what is the
gentleman's name? You know him, sir; he lives near
the river. Dear me! I forget the name of the street,"
and so on. Another man, named French, was also
a super at some theatre. He would, if asked to
stand with folded arms, consider it incumbent on him
to at once assume the scowl and scornful look with
which the stage bravo invariably regards "yon beardless boy!" It is related of him that on one occasion
he had a part in some piece of one line only, "My
lord, the carriage waits." At rehearsal it was found
necessary, for some exigency of the drama, to alter
this to "My lord, the carriage awaits your pleasure."

"Great heavens! *more study!*" was his exclama-
tion on being told this. "James Wood, Royal
Academy Model, suitable for the Georges," was
the card of a man whose head was so perfectly bald

AN OLD MODEL.

that he could wear any kind of wig. Occasionally
gentlemen of reduced circumstances, if one might
believe their own statements, were to be found in
the ranks of the models. One of these sat to me.
His name was Gordon; he had been an officer in

the Light Dragoons, and the fact of his speaking much better English than most models gave some colour to his assertion. He sat well and steadily, but was so small that all my costumes were a world too wide for him. I'm afraid I used to "chaff" him unmercifully on his leanness ; would make doggerel verses on it, and sing them to him ; or bring some of the children's clothes, and ask if he thought *they* would fit him. One day while sitting to a brother painter, after relating some more than usually out-rageous act or saying of mine, he said with much energy, " Sir, there are moments when I should like to strangle Mr. Marks!" At another time, the day being warm, the same artist sent Gordon to a neighbouring "pub" for a pot of beer. No-thing loth, he quickly returned, and as he placed the foaming tankard on the table observed, " Things have come to a pretty pass indeed, when an officer of the 14th Light Dragoons has to fetch his own beer!" But the most remarkable model I have known was one Campbell, a man of considerable natural gifts, but with no education save that which he had obtained from his mother's "horn-book" (the first book for children, so called from its cover being of horn). Campbell's vanity was inordinate but amusing. He began life as a shoemaker, but having injured one of his hands, had drifted into being a porter, and finally a model. Opinions as to

his personal appearance were divided ; some painters
considered him frightfully ugly ; others found that
his face and form were "full of character."   He
sat to me for my first picture, and was somewhat

STUDIES FOR FIGURES IN "THE JESTER'S TEXT."

uneasy, until I told him he might talk as much as
he liked, so long as he retained the position.   He
readily availed himself of this permission.   " I don't
know, sir," he began, "if I shall offend you, like I
did another gentleman I was a setting to last week.

We was talking about the Psalms of David, and I said as I didn't believe as David wrote 'em. I'm not a going to say but what he might have lent his name to 'em, or they might have been published

STUDIES FOR FIGURES IN "THE JESTER'S TEXT."

under his sanction, but I don't believe them psalms, as contains finer poetry than Shakespeare, Milton, Homer, Dante, and Virgil, and the whole lot on 'em put together, was ever written by a freebooter, a man who fell in love with another's wife, and placed her husband in the fore-front of the hottest battle, so as to get him out of the way! I don't believe he wrote 'em, no more than I believe John Bunyan wrote the 'Holy War.' I don't say nothing about the 'Pilgrim's Progress'—any fool could write that; but to tell me that Bunyan, a travelling tinker, a drunkard, a liar and swearer, could write that book, which shows knowledge of every rank and station in life, from the king upon his throne down to the head-borough—why, the military knowledge in that book alone would take the Duke o' Wellington to write! I say I don't believe it, no more than I believe that the psalms was written by David!" and so on *da capo*. On one occasion Campbell met the great Duke himself, an incident which will best be described in his own words. "I'd been to Apsley House to fetch away a picture that had been sent to him to look at. I was wrapping (pronounced ropping) it up in the green baize in the hall, when the Dook passes by and says, 'Oh, you've come from Messrs. Blank for that picture.' 'Yes, sir,' I says, and with that he touches his hat with his forefinger and walks out and gets on his horse. When he was gone, a man in black, his butler or valley-de-sham, I suppose, comes up to me, and he says, 'Do you know who you was a-speaking to just now?'—'Yes,' I says, 'I does. Arthur Wellesley, better known as the Duke of

Wellington.'—'Then why didn't you say *your grace* to him?' he says. 'Grace!' says I, 'what should I say grace for? There ain't no banquet spread here, is there? Where's the wiands? I called him Sir, the proper title between man and man.'—'Well,' he says, 'you're a rum kind of customer, you are. What do you call the Dook?'—'What do I call him?' I says, 'a wholesale carcase-butcher, that's what I calls him.'—'Well,' he says, 'suppose I was to write and tell your master of this?'—'Write and tell him,' I says, 'I'll take the letter myself. Now just look at his career,' I says. 'First of all, he goes to France to learn the art of war; after that he goes to India and kills thousands of the natives as was only defending their country, and at last fights the very country where he learnt the art of war, and kills thousands and thousands more. A wholesale carcase-butcher, that's what I calls him!'"

Campbell was a versifier, and when I married, wrote a special Epithalamium, which he brought neatly stitched in whitey-brown paper. If the tropes and images were more trite than original, at least the lines scanned, and bore a strong resemblance to those of Sternhold and Hopkins or Tate and Brady. At the birth of a child he would offer a congratulatory ode, nor was his Muse so far removed from all things sublunary as to prevent his acceptance of the humble honorariun of half-a-crown for these lucubrations.   In the days when Napoleon

THE TINKER.

threatened the invasion of England with his flat-bottomed boats, Campbell was a volunteer, and, like the immortal Jingle, would "bang the field-piece—twang the lyre." His martial ardour found vent in versification. As I have always had a fair verbal memory, I remember portions of some of these impassioned odes, and am thus enabled to present the reader with a sample.

> To grin at our snug little island of fame,
> Napoleon of France, when to Calais he came,
> His glass from his pocket beginning to draw,
> Was struck with amaze when Old England he saw.
>
> Britannia she sat on the white cliffs herself,
> But needed no spy-glass to look at that elf;
> She sat on the spot, by her Shakespeare renowned,
> Where Dover below by its summit is crowned.
>
> " I wonder," said she, " what that simpleton's doing ? "
> Replied Liberty, " Sister, he's plotting your ruin ! "
> " Is he so ? " said Britannia, " then let him plot on,
> I'm more than a match for that desperate Don.
>
> " Let him talk as he likes of his flat-bottomed boats,
> But our navy shall sink every vessel that floats;
> Let him come if he likes, for his boasting who cares ?
> Ere he gives us the skins, he must slaughter the bears ! "

The last sittings Campbell gave to me were for a figure in my picture

> "Hark! hark! the dogs do bark,
>   The beggars are coming to town," &c.,

exhibited at the Academy in 1865. He eventually

went into "the house," and would call now and then,
looking clean and neat in his brown coat and waist-
coat with brass buttons, and was grateful for a little
tea and tobacco or the eleemosynary shilling.　He
died at last in Gray's Inn Workhouse, chiefly of old
age, painlessly and in peace.

ST STEPHEN'S HALL,
PALACE CHAMBERS,
9 BRIDGE ST. WESTMINSTER. SW.

THE COMMITTEE OF THE
St STEPHEN'S ART SOCIETY
beg to invite

and friend,
to a
SOIRÉE
IN THE GALLERY
ON THE EVENING OF THE
9th NOVR 1881.
From
8 to 12.

MORNING DRESS.　　SMOKING AFTER 10.

CHAPTER XXI

BAMPTON

"YOU have a very bad cough, sir."—"It is the best I have," I answered apologetically. "Have you taken advice about it?"—"The best obtainable," said I, "if by best we understand the most expensive."—"Bronchial?" he inquired. "I rather think it's stomach," replied I. "And you take nothing for it?"—"Not now," I answered. "I took advice, as I told you, and have since taken bronchial troches, cough lozenges, and lung tonics by the hundredweight—balsams pectoral, of aniseed, and delusive mixtures by the gallon, but without result. I have been advised to try change of climate, to go to the Isle of Wight, the Riviera,

WAITING FOR THE DOCTOR.
By F. J. Skill.

Nismes, and other salubrious spots ; but not having the constitution of a confirmed invalid, have always been afraid to make the experiment."

This conversation took place in a railway carriage some years ago between a clergyman of curiously cadaverous aspect and myself. I was on my way to Bampton in North Devon, of which place I shall have more to say presently. By the sympathetic expression of this clergyman's countenance, he evidently thought my days were numbered in the land, and if my image has ever crossed his mental retina since we conversed together, it must have been as that of a florid corpse. He was not the only one who has wasted kind but needless sympathy on me. My relatives have taken deep interest in my solitary ailment, which is the more to be wondered at, as the probabilities are that I shall not leave them piles of wealth at my decease. I make no apology for calling the attention of my readers to my complaint. Being my only one, I am naturally a little proud of it. It is my trade-mark (copyright reserved), my distinguishing badge. Its sound is recognised by my friends afar off. By a judicious use of it I can avoid a troublesome argument, assist to bring to a conclusion the dreary speech of a bore at a public dinner, or escape the tedium of a lengthy lecture by an aggravated specimen of its distressing symptoms, and leave the hall followed by the pitying looks of the tender-hearted fair.

The learned physician whom I consulted in the infancy of my cough assured me that it was a mistake to suppose that a cough was an entity; there was no such thing (I wished that he could have had mine for just five minutes). I was stripped to the waist, punched, pummelled, and pulled about. At the end of this athletic performance, I had the gratification of being told that my heart and lungs were sound. The physician advised me to go at once to Hastings, bade me farewell as he pocketed his fee, and I went on my way and saw him no more. I was reminded of all this some years after when staying at Bampton at my son-in-law's. I was playing in the garden with my grandson, a smart little chap between five and six years of age then. When I began coughing, he came running up to me, calling out, "Here, grandad! smell this flower, and see if it wont disinfect you of that nasty cough." I smiled as I thought the prescription of the child was as likely to be as efficacious as anything that had been told me by the disciple of Æsculapius.

Every one must have noticed, in his wanderings through the land of his birth, how the local guide-books, with unconscious humour, will vaunt the praises of the place they describe, on the *lucus a*

non lucendo principle. Thus, if a neighbourhood
is devoid of trees, the guide-book will allude to the
luxurious vegetation with enthusiasm, will magnify
a stream into a river, a mole-hill into a mountain,
with other vagaries of imaginative description too
numerous to mention. I stayed with a friend once
at a village called Liphook in Hants. In a weak
moment I had listened to one who represented it as
affording good opportunities for the painter who
sought a change from studying the professional
model, in the contemplation and portrayal of landscape. But there are no landscapes of any beauty,
and the surrounding buildings are of the latest and
most vulgar type. " Jubilee Cottages " and " Ter-
races " meet you at every turn. What landscape
there is, is invisible to the pedestrian, by reason
of the roads having high hedges. It is like walking in a magnified Hampton Court maze. The
guide-book to this district is more than usually
delusive ; it is written by one who waxes eloquent over beauties that have no existence. True,
it rained each day we were there—it was the wet
summer of 1888—and this may have helped to pre-
judice the place in our estimation. At the end of
the fourth day, we could stand it no longer, and,
damp and disconsolate, took train to town ; but not
before we had relieved our feelings by some doggrel
verses, which, not being of a complimentary char-

acter, will be looked for in vain in the visitors' book of the Anchor Hotel.

Bampton, though what most people would call a village, is dignified, by virtue of possessing a Local Board, with the title of town. It borders on Exmoor, is seven miles north of Tiverton, and very near the boundary-line which divides North Devon from West Somerset.

It stands on a stream called by courtesy the river Batherm, a tributary of the Exe, into which it flows about a mile below the town, after winding alongside the Exe Valley Railway through a deep and precipitous valley, the woody cliffs of which remind one somewhat, though on a smaller scale, of the valley of the Dart.

Bampton, I am informed, "strikes the visitor irresistibly as being an ancient town;" the houses, streets, and all the surroundings proclaim it "of another day," while "the quaintness and serenity pervading the whole place would suggest to the city man a pleasant idea of repose."

I may be singular, but my first visit to Bampton gave me the idea, which I have since seen no reason to modify, that it is essentially modern and common-place; the houses and streets are tame and characterless. The town lies in a hole seen from the hills above; its colour is dull grey. The house roofs are of bluish slate, very few being thatched; the walls of grey stone, with exceptional cases of whitewash. If Bampton is of "another day," that day must be the day before

THE ANGEL INN, BAMPTON.

yesterday. The "quaintness" I have been unable to discover; but if by "serenity" is meant dulness, then I cordially agree. A capital place for quiet, but any one going to stay there should bring some occupation with him, if he would not die of boredom and *ennui*.

BAMPTON IN WET WEATHER.

The scenery, or, as I should prefer to call it, the landscape to the east of Bampton is un-picturesque. Huge shapeless hills are divided by hedges into fields of every form and different coloured crops, suggestive of the old-fashioned counterpane on a gigantic scale. To the west, however, the landscape gradually improves, developing into scenery of great beauty at a little distance.

Bampton has, of course, a history and many legends, most of which must be accepted with some degree of caution. The earliest military transaction among the Saxons connected with Devon is a battle at Bampton (Beaudune), in which Cynegilous (a good name that!), King of the West Saxons, vanquished the Britons with great slaughter about the year A.D. 614. The barony of Bampton was the property of the king in Edward the Confessor's time. William the Conqueror gave it to Walter de Douay. It then passed into the Paganell family, and from them to the Cogans. Richard Cogan was licensed by the Crown to castellate his mansion-house at Bampton in the fourteenth century. The natives show you a steep-sided circular mound, with a clump of fir-trees, in which is a rookery, at the summit, which mound they tell you was the keep of Bampton Castle. There are no remains of any buildings, but that there was a castle somewhere about is proved incontestably by the fact of a Castle Inn, Castle Street, and a house

called Castle Grove, existing in the immediate
vicinity. Somewhat to my surprise, I have been
unable to discover any record of this castle ever
having been besieged by Cromwell, or of Queen
Elizabeth occupying its best bedroom, or even
that at the Castle Inn.

The inhabitants boast of their chalybeate saline
spring. Having tested it, I can testify that it
has what Sam Weller described as a flavour of
flat irons, and a red deposit soon accumulates
in an earthen mug or other vessel in which any
of the water has been left. Proud as they are
of this spring and its medicinal merits, I never
saw any Bamptonians drinking it, which shows
that they are a generous and unselfish people.
They would not rob the visitor of any beneficial
effects that might accrue to his system by imbibing
the waters.

The real attractions of Bampton are its annual
fair on the last Thursday in October, when dealers
from all parts of the kingdom are attracted by
the number of Exmoor ponies driven there—
little creatures not very much larger than a full-
grown Newfoundland dog, but of great strength
and very sure-footed. The town and district are
beloved by sportsmen for the meets of the
Devon and Somerset staghounds gathered in
the neighbourhood for hunting the red deer, and

of the fox and otter hounds.   The angler can
gratify his love of sport in immediate proximity
to the town, by the banks of the Exe and its
tributaries, where trout and salmon are to be
found in great numbers.   But these delights

UNDER THE YEW-TREE IN THE DOCTOR'S GARDEN.

all pale before the attraction that Bampton has
for me personally.   A friend of mine once said
that pater-familiarity breeds contempt.   I hope I
may not be an object for "scorn to point his
slow unmoving finger at" by confessing that I
like the little Devon town chiefly because it is

the home of my married daughter, my son-in-law, the doctor of the town (Thomas Guinness by name), their two children, and my grandchildren, boy and girl. Often do I run down there when change or quiet are needed. Not that quiet is

FROM THE CHURCHYARD, BAMPTON.

always to be had in Bampton. In the year 1887, thinking to escape the noise and excitement of the Jubilee celebration in town, I fled to Bampton only to exchange one set of noises for another, though much was new and not devoid of interest. I wrote an account of the day's festivities and rejoicings for the *Tiverton Gazette*, of which the following is an extract :—

A LONDONER'S IMPRESSIONS OF BAMPTON JUBILEE.

"The day broke fairly and softly on the morning of the 21st. Awaking about four o'clock, I opened my window, and was sensible of a balmy though somewhat keen air and a bright cloudless sky. Bampton still slept, but birds and animals had already begun to 'jubilate.' From each farm-yard the domestic cocks vied with each other in loudly proclaiming the auspicious morn. Rooks, thrushes, ducks, and blackbirds joined in the chorus, emphasised at regular intervals by the monotonous note of the cuckoo, and (*absit omen*) the bassoon-like bray of a wakeful and festive donkey. At eight o'clock the bells of the old church rang out a merry peal, and Bampton, which over-night had shown little or no evidence of anything unusual occurring, was found in the morning to have blossomed into extensive decoration. The conventional wreaths and flags were abundantly evident, but a novel and effective feature was made by large boughs of oak-trees placed on the foot-way and leaning against the walls of the houses. Soon after ten, the population began to assemble for a special service in the parish church. After some

delay in marshalling, a procession was formed and
marched to the church.   First came the brass
band of the town, and the C. Company of Devon
Rifles ; representatives of various trades followed,
each bearing the implements of his craft, as in the
Guild processions of olden days.

" Members of the Benefit Clubs, wearing scarves
of fearful and wonderful colours, only to be seen on
similar occasions, came next.   To these succeeded
the parishioners (male only) ; manor officials, includ-
ing ale-tasters and scavengers ; the Celebration
Committee, churchwardens, &c., while the rear was
brought up by the Vicar and assistant clergy,
escorted on the one hand by the serjeants and
corporals of the Ordnance Survey, on the other by
the whole of the local Devonshire constabulary in
the person of Serjeant Vole.   The service was
simple and solemn, the anthem, effectively rendered,
was listened to by a congregation far larger than
any hitherto remembered by that ubiquitous bore
'the oldest inhabitant.'

"The service ended, the procession left the church
in the same order as before, and, with band playing
and crowd following, ascended to Brickdown field,
where royal salutes were fired with a small cannon,
while the volunteers contributed *feux de joie*.
Noise of all kinds is the concomitant of rejoicing,
and there were few minutes in the day in which

the echoes of the hills were not called on to re-
spond to the discharge of firearms, the ringing of
bells, and the striking and sonorous strains of the
Bampton band.   But the great event of the day
was a dinner for the male parishioners, preparations for which had been taking place all the
morning.   In the centre of the principal street, an
all but interminable line of tables was arranged ; the
seats comprised every variety of bench and form.
The effect of the white-covered tables and vases of
flowers, the festoons of flags and foliage, backed
up by the massive hills relieved against a clear
blue sky, was picturesque.   A blazing sun and a
strong east wind made the heat intense, the dust
a caution.   Boys with a sense of the ridiculous
attempted to allay the latter by a liberal use of
watering-pots : as well attempt to empty an ocean
with a spoon.   And now the tables are served ;
mighty joints of beef, covered with newspapers to
protect them from sun and dust, make the tables
literally groan ; at a given signal, cheers for the Queen
are raised ; the Vicar asks a blessing on the viands,
and we sit down to a collation, nominally cold, but
actually the hottest at which I ever assisted.   Of
shade there was none ; the sun shone hotter and
hotter, and the reflections from the white houses and
dusty road intensified the heat.   But what matter ?
We had determined to enjoy ourselves, and enjoy

ourselves we did. What though the heat dried up the salad, parched the mustard, crusted the bread, and tended to flatten the beer; while the gusty wind with clouds of dust converted our roast into powdered beef? Each one stuck manfully to his task, and contentedly consumed his liberal

THOUGH QUAINT MY SHAPE
MY HEART IS TRUE ; —

1885.

A HAPPY NEW YEAR
TO YOURS AND YOU!

allowance of beef, beer, and pudding. The meal ended, it was a sight to be not easily forgotten, how, perspiring alike with loyalty and liquor, we sang the National Anthem in unison, if a little out of tune, to the accompaniment of the ever-ready and untiring band. The female parishioners were not forgotten in the general joy, and though the coarser pleasures of beef and pudding were denied them, they were amply indemnified by a bountiful supply of the more feminine refreshments of tea and cake in the National Schoolroom. The latter part of the day was devoted to athletic sports, which call for no particular remark. As darkness gathered round it was impressive to watch the bonfires lighting up from hill to hill and beacon answering beacon as far as the eye could reach. Such a combination of nature and art gave the neighbourhood illuminations of a grandeur which London might envy but could not equal."

CHAPTER XXII

BIRDS—THE ZOO

FROM a child I was fond of animals. I cannot remember the time when, with but one or two exceptions, my sympathies were not always with them. Affection for birds, always present but dormant, did not develop in a graphic or pictorial sense till I was nearly thirty. For the early drawings I made of birds, which a fond mother preserved—and some of which I possess now—are utterly devoid of promise or of precocious skill. They evidence industry and the wish to be "always at it"—nothing beyond. As the standard of technical excellence in art is raised to a higher level year by year, so the child of to-day draws

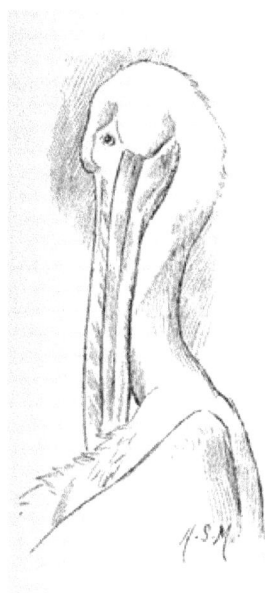

better than the child of forty years ago.   And
what wonderful books are made for our grandchildren !   The best writers, the best artists work
for them.   It is impossible for a child now-a-days
not to be influenced by the admirable specimens
of draughtsmanship he sees in most illustrated
books and periodicals.   A child's book to-day is
a work of art.   In my mind's eye I can just dimly
see a picture-book I had presented me on an early
birthday.   It was an illustrated alphabet with the
fine old crusted rhymes—

> A was an archer, who shot at a frog ;
> B was a butcher, who had a great dog, &c., &c.

This was anything but a work of art.   As I
look at it now, in fancy, with the eye of childhood,
but with the judgment of a greybeard, I should
describe the drawing as rude and the colour in-
solent.   The illustrations were characterised by
ignorance and vulgarity.   I doubt if anything *quite*
so bad as this little volume could be obtained now
for love or money.   Though digressing from the
subject with which I, started, I cannot, before
returning to the birds, resist this opportunity of
recording my admiration of the high state of excellence that has been reached by "black and white"
as illustrative art in this country.   Not only in
children's books, but in books for adults and in

many periodicals do we find art of the highest
excellence and technical skill. Sir John Gilbert,
who by his genius and example so promoted the
interests of illustrated journalism, may be looked on
as the father of that numerous and brilliant band
of young artists who are daily giving examples of
their great talent to the world. He is the
parent stem of which the younger branches have
ramified in so many directions. The *Daily
Graphic* is to me a daily marvel. What precision
of drawing in the illustrations, what economy of
line, so much suggested by the fewest possible
touches, and what judicious knowledge shown in
leaving the blank paper as a means of effect! And
when it is considered that many of these drawings
are made over-night, to appear next morning in
the journal, I marvel still more. Some good-
natured friend will think I am puffing the journal
and the artists who work on it, though I have not
mentioned one of their names; so let us get back
to the birds. It is pleasant to reflect that I can
praise or abuse them without exciting any one's
susceptibilities.

I have said I was about thirty years of age
before I thought of birds from a pictorial point
of view. It was on one of several Continental
trips with Calderon that this idea was aroused.
In the autumn of 1863 we went to the South of

France, with some half-defined notion of staying
in some town and painting there.   We travelled
from place to place, but found no rest for our feet.
From one cause or another, none suited; there was
a difficulty about getting rooms with a suitable
light, or the rents were too high, and after an
absence of about three weeks I was beginning to
get home-sick.   I never confessed this weakness
to Calderon, but, accustomed to study faces as he
was and is, he no doubt saw what was the matter.
Among other towns, we stopped a night or two
at Ligugé, Bordeaux, Carcassone, Montpellier, and
Nismes.   Our short stay at this last-named town
still dwells "in the book and volume of my brain,"
for it was here that I learned to look upon the
British invalid with veneration, not unmixed with
wonder, somewhat akin to the feeling I had on first
seeing Sandow and other muscular athletes.   In
the simple language of my diary, I find recorded
"Nismes, awfully cold here!   Wind fearful.
A March wind in London a mere zephyr by comparison!"   The mistral was blowing its hardest.
Walking was out of the question; no amount of exercise seemed to increase the temperature of our
bodies.   The greater part of our time was spent in
cafés playing billiards, where the air, if close, was
at least warm.   And this wind, which made us shiver,
nipped our young bloods (I am speaking of thirty

years ago) and reddened our noses, was the breath
of life to the invalid. They told me colonies of

STORKS.

invalids, chiefly English, resided here, and lived
and throve in the chilly blast which would send

to the grave the man of ordinarily robust health.
Having been thoroughly refrigerated at Nismes,
we got thawed at Arles, where Calderon obtained
material for several pictures, into which he introduced pretty Arlesiennes.
We went back to Nismes,
staying as short a time as
possible ; thence to Macon
and Paris, for we had now
determined on returning
home.

Leaving Paris, we stayed
a night at Amiens at the
Hotel du Rhin.   It was
while walking early the next
morning in the hotel garden
that I suddenly came upon
two ordinary white storks
(*Ciconia alba*) at liberty,
taking, as I was, a stroll
before breakfast.   I was
fascinated at once, and followed them, sketch-book in
hand.   That habit of standing on one leg, the
dainty, stealthy, striding walk, the quaint clattering of the mandibles, and a certain weird, almost
human expression, as if "the soul of our gran-
dam might haply inhabit a bird," were all very

DESIGN FOR FRETWORK DOOR-
PLATE

novel and delightful to me. I really believe, in thinking of that morning, that these storks impressed me more than all the churches, town-halls, and even (I blush to confess it) the picture-galleries that we entered. Since then the storks, the cranes, the herons, and all the long-legged birds, have been special favourites of mine, and in many respects I prefer them to the human model. They are less vain and less greedy—they don't bore you with their conceit, or with long gossiping stories, without point, of the artists to whom they have sat. Nor do they expect you to be talkative and amusing for their benefit, or require seven shillings a day and a hot lunch as a slight recognition of their invaluable services.

DOOR-PLATE FRETWORK.

Towards the end of the year 1888, the Fine Art Society proposed a scheme of holding an exhibition of "Birds" at their rooms in Bond Street. The idea recommended itself to me, for it might be successful, having the element of

novelty to recommend it, and novelty is beloved
by the public.   So in the following May, having
finished my work for the Academy and other
Exhibitions, I set to, and became a frequent
haunter of the Zoo, and soon established intimate
relations with "my feathered friends" and the
keepers who looked after them.   Many of the
birds, I believe, learned actually to know me,
and watched my proceedings with evident curiosity.
Some of the parrots, with their monkey-like mis-
chievous nature, resented having their portraits
taken, and the moment that pencil and sketch-
book appeared, became very restless and fidgety
or indulged in shrieking remonstrances.   "Not
to-day, thank you!" they would scream to me, and
if, inadvertently, I had left my water-bottle within
reach of one of them, he would incontinently tip it
over and spill the contents with malicious glee.
Other less excitable natures resigned themselves
to fate, and became profoundly indifferent, regarding me with extreme contempt from the corners
of their half-closed eyes.   But of all the birds who
entirely ignore you, commend me to the eagle,
who won't even look at you; or to the adjutant-
stork, who looks wiser than any bird ever was, and
is the best sitter of them all.   On what weighty
problems is he pondering, in what profound reflections engaged, as he stands there, often on one leg

only, motionless as a statue, for a quarter of an hour at a time?

The parrot-house is a good winter studio, kept at a comfortable uniform temperature. The heat in summer makes it impracticable for any one not blessed with the constitution of a salamander, and the glaring untempered sunshine is distracting. The walls, coloured with that vile French blue so much affected by the modern house-painter, or decorator, as he persists in calling himself, form the worst possible background for parrots and macaws. And the noise, as every one knows, is deafening; the house is a Pandemonium of discordant shrieks, squeals, squalls, and screeches! Visitors open the door, look in for a moment, and retire with their fingers stopping their ears. Artists subject to head-ache are driven to frenzy and despair, and though I have at various times passed so many hours among the parrots and cockatoos, I have never got accustomed to the frightful racket in which they so gleefully indulge.

The Zoo has its drawbacks. Go to whatever part you will, you are never safe from the curious inquisitive visitor and the school-children. People who would perhaps hesitate to read a private letter you were writing do not scruple to look over your shoulder at the sketch you are making. The curious one is followed by others, and you

will soon be surrounded by a gaping crowd; for
not the latest addition to the menagerie has anything like the attraction that is possessed by an
artist sketching.   You rise from your camp-stool
and stand to your work; the hint is too subtle to
be taken; not one budges.   Pretending to sharpen
your pencil or to clean your colour-box are feeble

Boat-bill.
(S. America.)

subterfuges that are of no avail.   I found, after
employing many dodges, that there were only two
ways of dispersing these troublesome people: one,
to shut up your sketch-book, and, keeping a sharp
look-out on your "traps," retire for a while to a
more removed ground.   But this takes time.   The

best way of all is to rise promptly from your seat,
turn your back on the creature you are drawing,
and your face to the foe ; this bothers the loafers,
who retire slowly and sadly.   I have never known
this plan fail.   Another type of visitor is the
question-asker, with a thirst for information and
no bump of locality.   He has his plan and catalogue
of the gardens, but is unable to discover the site
of the reptile-house, or on which side of "the
tunnel" the elephants are housed.   Or he may
want to leave the gardens altogether, and, with
the insatiable appetite of the sight-seer, wish to
visit as many shows as can be managed in the
twenty-four hours.   In this case he will ask you
the shortest route to the Tower, the Imperial
Institute, or the Aquarium, &c., &c., and expect
you to explain the various routes of 'bus and tram,
and indicate the nearest cab-rank or railway station.
Instances of this kind should be treated with an
assumed deafness.   It is the most efficacious remedy
and quite harmless.

As for the school-children of both sexes, who
swarm at the Zoo, it grieves me to say that they
are little short of offensive.   For children generally I have great love ; their outspokenness and
simplicity, freedom from humbug and hypocrisy,
their intense naturalness, in short, endear them to
me.   Perhaps I prefer them in detail rather than

in bulk.   An interminable band of boys or girls
trooping past the dens and cages, talking at the
highest pitch of their voices, the girls screaming
and laughing, the boys shouting and grating the
gravel with their iron-shod boots, however delightful as illustrating the health and happy carelessness
of childhood, is not a sight which causes delight
to the lover of peace and quiet.   The animals
don't like it, and the birds become nervous, excited,
and restless.   On they come, the dear little things,
not looking whither they are going.   Your camp-
stool and easel will be knocked over without a
word of apology, if you don't take the precaution
to rise and protect your property by the inter-
position of your body.   A stout figure, with a
weight of between twelve and thirteen stone, is
effectual in stemming the rushing tide of childhood.

On all days of the week except Saturday these
schools are admitted to the gardens free from nine
till twelve.   Printed papers are handed to the
teachers at the entrance-gates with instructions as
to the conduct and management of the children,
who are, or are supposed to be, under their control.
These instructions are all but disregarded in one
respect at least.   The children bring their dinners
with them, and litter the gardens with the greasy
papers that have served as wrappers of their food.

However "thick autumnal leaves that strow the brooks in Vallombrosa" may be, they cannot equal in numbers the dirty bits of newspaper which reduce grass and gravel to one uniform dingy tint. Men are told off, after the departure of the innocents, with picks and baskets to clear away these

A STUDY.

evidences of the feast. During the few minutes allotted for taking sustenance, I have observed the male and female teachers often derive more pleasant employment in mild flirtations with each other than in looking after their untidy pupils. But children are not the only offenders. The

sight of the great lawn on the morning succeeding
a Bank Holiday, covered with the debris of the
orgies of the day before, is enough to make the
hair of a Quaker stand on end. Greasy, ragged
papers, bottles whole or broken, glass or earthenware ; pipes, pewter pots, and all kinds of loathsome
litter, form abundant evidence of that English love
of neatness and order among the humbler orders
(if I may venture to use the term), of which we
read so often in gushing leaders and see so seldom
in actual life.

But staring visitors and noisy children are harmless and of little annoyance compared with the flies
which infest every part of the Zoo, and are to me a
maddening nuisance. Whether in the open air or
under cover, the fiendish fly pursues me with relent-
less pertinacity, regarding me apparently as corrupt
matter, that must be removed by its repeated efforts.
It is humiliating to be regarded even by the fly
as so much garbage or carrion. What particular
quality there can be about my skin that has a
fascination for the fly I have never been able to
ascertain. My epidermis is neither thin nor delicate ;
but the fly loses no opportunity of attempting to
puncture it, and frequently succeeds. It is strange
that while a martyr to the fly, I am on the best
terms with the flea. I never remember being bitten
by the flea, though it has had ample opportunities

of sucking my blood. In the double-bedded rooms
of country inns, my friends have risen in the morning spotted like the leopard, while I have left my
couch unscarred and unscathed. On the Continent,
where the flea is of larger size, more vindictive and
bloodthirsty in nature, and vastly more numerous
than in our happy clime, I have slept soundly, my
body unbitten. I know of no remedy against the
savage onslaughts of the fly that is not disagreeable
and impracticable. The oils of eucalyptus or of
cloves rubbed on the hands will protect them, but
no one with the greatest indifference to personal
appearance can anoint his head and face with oil.
I have a strong aversion to grease, and the odour of
either oil is by no means pleasant. The fly exhibits
diabolical ingenuity in its attacks. It will wait till
you are engaged on a part of your drawing requiring particular care or steadiness of hand ; then rush
at, sting you, and be off again ere you can seize it.
Its most maddening device is to approach silently,
when off your guard, and make you aware of its
disgusting presence by buzzing and booming violently in the orifice of the ear. The sound lasts
less than a minute, but during that time you endure
years of agony. The hated insect flies away, buzzing in derision at the impotence of your wrath and
the strength of your language.

It is many years since I first visited the Zoo,

but I cannot discover that the intelligence of the average visitor has reached a higher level during that period. The notions about the food proper and natural for bird or beast are still hazy and undefined. A twopenny or fourpenny paper-bag, procured from the refreshment-bar, filled with yesterday's pastry, and labelled "Food for the animals," is regarded as capable of supplying every want. Bread also is considered a universal pabulum. It is offered to the polar bear and the seal alike. I have seen nuts presented to the Pondicherry vulture, sponge-cakes to the crested eagle, and there is little doubt that, were it not for the protection of plate-glass, pastry would be offered to the pythons. Why not, when gingerbread-nuts and peppermint-drops are thought to be the daintiest delicacies that can be given to the larger carnivora?

But the most comical instance of ignorance as to what creatures will eat occurred one day in the Fish-house. The keeper was engaged in filling a hole in the floor of a cage with that granulated burnt red clay (called ballast, I think). To him enters a gentleman who asks, "Is that the stuff you feed the penguins with?" This was not said in chaff or sarcastically. If ever there was a face that showed its owner was guileless of humour, that inquirer had it.

Remarks made on one's work are sometimes not flattering to vanity. When one has advanced pretty far with a study, to hear 'Arry say to his mate, "What bird is 'e a-doin' of, Bill?" is amusing though not complimentary. I have often smiled to think I was credited with some power of keeping birds still, by the remarks made by different people, because the specimen I was drawing happened to be quiescent at the moment they passed. A girl once said, "Do they never move?" I could only ask her in return if *she* never moved. Venerable ladies exclaim, "Ah! pretty creature! doesn't he seem to know he's sitting for his picture!" But it was reserved for a man, with the superior intelligence of the sex, to ask, "Do you hypnotise the birds?" I had rather not print my reply.

Notwithstanding all the little annoyances and inconveniences of the Zoo, it is a most charming place for either work or idleness. There are few days, except those on which the fog-demon is abroad, that the ardent enthusiast cannot draw there. Numerous sheds and houses afford protection from rain. Defiance can always be bidden to cold in the comfortable temperature of the parrot-house, if only you button your coat and keep your mouth closed in coming out into the frosty air. In fine summer weather the whole area of the gardens, made brilliant by the colour of the flower-beds glowing in the warm sunshine, is a vast studio. When the heat is too enervating, relief from the sun's rays can always be had by sitting in the broad shade of the spreading chestnut-tree which is opposite the vulture's aviary, and close to the railing which surrounds the Three Island Pond. After long experience, I find this is the coolest place in the gardens. If ever so little air is in motion elsewhere, it becomes a breeze under the tree. The path in which it stands is out of the beaten track of the sight-seer, so that you may enjoy almost uninterrupted solitude while you smoke a contemplative pipe. Your eye is refreshed by the colour of the flowers in mingling sun and shade, and your ear conscious of the stillness being pleasantly broken by the distant trumpet-like cry of the cranes, the faint wailing of the seagulls, or the low muffled thunder which comes from the Lion-house.

I was very congenially occupied, either at the gardens or at home, from the beginning of May till nearly the middle of October 1889, in working for my Bird Exhibition, wrote a little preface for the catalogue, designed the private view card, and drew a poster to be carried as an advertisement by the "sandwich-men." On October 21st my show of " Birds," or " Poultry," as it was called by a facetious Academician, was opened to the public, and remained on view for six weeks. All doubts, in which I had so often indulged, with regard to its success, were entirely dispelled before the Exhi-

MR H·STACY·MARKS begs to invite

TO A PRIVATE VIEW
OF
SKETCHES AND DRAWINGS OF

BIRDS,

ON OCTOBER 18th 1890,
at the FINE ART SOCIETY'S
ROOMS,
148 NEW BOND ST.
W.

PRIVATE VIEW CARD TO THE SECOND EXHIBITION.

bition had been opened a week. As I had ventured to hope, the novelty of its character attracted the public, who showed the pleasantest appreciation, by purchasing nearly every exhibit.

The critics were kind, lenient, and even flattering.
What more could I wish for? Here was both
praise and pudding. Moreover, not only were the
greater part of the birds, from parrot to penguin,
disposed of at the Fine Art Society's rooms, but
the demand continuing, I worked after the close
of the Exhibition till all but the end of December
to supply that demand. The daily routine was :—
After breakfast, cab to the Zoo at nine, worked
(generally in the parrot-house) for four hours. Cab
home — lunch. Afternoon, walk — Bond Street.
Left drawing made that morning at the Fine Art
Society's — Club — Home. Not infrequently the
drawing made in the morning would be sold in the
afternoon. This provoked my facetious confrère
to make a caricature sketch of the writer standing
at a shop-door on which was inscribed the legend
"Poultry is cheap to-day!" It is in no spirit of
vain boasting that I say I was very gratified with
the financial results of this enterprise, however
much I might have been disappointed had I been
a music-hall artiste. A second Exhibition, held
at the Society's rooms in the following year,
though it contained many more examples, was not
proportionately so successful as the first. Second
attempts seldom are. The freshness and novelty
had diminished, and this may account in some
measure for the falling off; but the falling off was

not sufficient to cause dissatisfaction with the general results.

On looking back to the time devoted to getting together these Exhibitions, passed as so much of it was in the fresh air and in work so congenial, demanding just sufficient sense of labour and solicitude to make it exhilarating rather than exhausting, it seems to be one of the pleasantest passages of my life.

POSTER OF MY EXHIBITION AT BOND STREET.

POSTER OF FIRST BOND STREET EXHIBITION.

CHAPTER XXIII

RUSKIN

IT was in 1856 that I first saw Mr. Ruskin in the flesh, but it was not for some years after that our acquaintance ripened into friendship. Commencing in 1855, he published an annual pamphlet entitled "Notes on some of the Principal Pictures in the Royal Academy, and the Society of Painters in Water Colours," in which the criticism was certainly "new," and in some instances distinctly trenchant. Without any respect for names merely as names, the critic said what he believed to be the truth in the boldest and most fearless manner. Great

was the fluttering caused in artistic dovecotes by
the appearance of these "Notes." They were
eagerly looked for, and as eagerly purchased, and
no doubt considerably influenced the work of many
of the younger painters. Mr. Ruskin had before
taken up the cudgels, with signal effect, in defence
of the Pre-Raphaelite brethren, when they were
attacked, ridiculed, and vilified by the writers and
by some of the painters of the day. His bias
in favour of that school was evident now, when
so much careless, sloppy, and incompetent work
abounded in our Exhibitions (always, of course, with
notable exceptions), when men still painted, as
Herbert said, "with the heels, or with the elbows,
in a slapdash manner." Mr. Ruskin exerted his
influence as strongly and conscientiously as he
could against all that was careless or insincere,
affected or flippant. *Punch*, reflecting always the
age and body of the time, its form and pressure, gave
utterance to the wail of the Royal Academician—

> "I takes and paints,
>   Hears no complaints,
>   I'm sold before I'm dry.
>   When savage Ruskin
>   Sticks his tusk in,
>   Then nobody will buy!"

The "Notes" for the year 1856 I made the
subject of a little skit, with coloured caricatures of

the pictures, and parodies of Mr. Ruskin's style in writing and critical views. I bound the few pages roughly together, for the thing never got beyond manuscript form, but it enjoyed a very large private circulation at many a conversazione and assembly where artists most do congregate. I had the precious work in my possession up to a few years ago, and would have liked to reproduce it, or at least some portion of it, but it has quite disappeared; search has been again and again made for it, but always with the same disappointing result. I can only conclude that some one, whose memory where books or umbrellas are concerned is a perfect blank, has forgotten to return it, or that it has been appropriated by one of those strangers who, without invitation, force their way into the studio on " Picture Sunday," become suddenly afflicted with kleptomania, and walk off with what unconsidered trifles they can "snap up." Anyhow, I never expect to see my " Notes " again.

To return to my story. At some gathering of artists, Woolner told me that he had mentioned my brochure to Mr. Ruskin, who immediately expressed a wish to see it. I posted it to him the next morning, with an explanatory line or two, which was promptly acknowledged by the great writer, who thanked me for sending him the " Notes," "and still more for the compliment of your knowing I should enjoy them." One or two other short communications of a complimentary nature I received from Mr. Ruskin I pasted in the cover of the little book, which makes the loss of it the more vexatious. Presently he wrote, "If you come down to the National Gallery any day, and ask the policeman for me, we may meet, and at least know each other's faces." I went, and found the eloquent exponent of Turner in rooms in the basement of the building, surrounded by piles of sketch-books and loose drawings by the master, which he was arranging, mounting, and framing, a congenial employment, a labour of love, to which he devoted months of time, with no recompense beyond the pleasure which the occupation afforded him. I can remember little of our conversation except that it was chiefly about Turner and his work. I had gone to the Gallery with an ill-defined feeling of awe of the great man I was about to see, but this was dissipated directly I had shaken hands with him. There was none of the posing of the genius ; I found him perfectly simple, unaffected, kindly, and human. After staying some while, Brett came in, when with mutual expressions of good-will we parted.

I don't know how it was, but I never corresponded again, so far as I recollect, with Mr. Ruskin until the Walker Exhibition was coming on, as described in a former chapter. After that we became intimate. He, Arthur and Mrs. Severn would dine with us occasionally when he was in town, and I, with my wife and two daughters, had several pleasant dinners and evenings at Herne Hill. (I think, as we have now become so friendly, I may drop the " Mr. " for the future.) On better acquaintance, I found Ruskin more natural, unaffected, and courteous than I had at first thought him. However heterodox some of my opinions on art may have seemed to him, he never showed the least irritation, but would smilingly put me right with a phrase half joke, half earnest. At the little diversions we made for his amusement after dinner he was the best and most easily amused man it was ever my lot to play the fool before. Only those who have had to sing a song, or give a recitation supposed to be of a humorous nature, before an audience as devoid of a sense of humour as any Ibsenite, know what a dreary, melancholy, uphill task it is. I would give him an imitation of the swell music-hall singer, his hat worn very much on one side, and requiring continual adjusting, flourishing his cane, and shooting his shirt-cuffs ; or of a fourth-rate actor, with his gushings and gurglings, which Ruskin would enjoy as much as, or more than a boy of to-day ; or we would give him a rendering of H. S. Leigh's song of " Uncle John," which eventually became his

household name.   One of my sons sang the air,
accompanied by a daughter on the piano, while

the other two boys and I performed a sort of
pantomime, which can only be described as idiotic.

To see "the Professor," as we then called him, clap his hands, and roll on his chair as his eyes were bedimmed with tears of laughter, was a sight to more than gratify the actors. The song itself, though perhaps not up to the intellectual level of " Daddy won't buy me a bow-wow," and other favourites of the music-hall stage, is not without wit and point. I give it here :—

UNCLE JOHN.

I never loved a dear gazelle,
In point of fact, I never tried ;
But had I known and loved one well,
I'm quite convinced it would have died.
My old and wealthy Uncle John
Has known me long, has loved me well,
Yet still he will go living on :
Ah ! would he were a young gazelle !

I never loved a tree or flower,
But, if I had, without a doubt
The frost or blight, the wind or show'r,
Would soon have come and snuff'd it out.
I've dearly loved my Uncle John
From childhood till the present hour ;
And yet he *will* go living on :
Ah ! would he were a tree or flow'r !

I've often heard how Death destroys
The good and pure when very young ;
He takes away dear little boys,
But spares the greatest rogues unhung :

Whene'er I meet my Uncle John
A solemn thought occurs to me :
If Uncle John keeps living on—
How wicked Uncle John must be !

I have often wondered how so firm and fast a friendship came to exist between a man of such wide and varied learning, of such great intellect, and myself. Perhaps the following passage from one of Ruskin's letters may help to explain the difficulty :—

" I greatly thank you also for the sentence in your letter about friendship. I do most seriously think that among all my friends there is none with whom I may have so complete sympathy. The differences between us seem to me never in the least *contrary*, but to be in each of us some speciality, which as it were goes out on the other side, while we can fit like hand and glove on the fitting side. My other friends fit more or less on many sides, but always with some bumps or grit in the way."

This is dated 1877, and on Christmas Eve in the same year he wrote thus :—

" Knowing you as I have learnt to do this year, adds a very broad 'bit of blue'* to my Christmas sky, and a very bright 'bit of red' to my Christmas holly-bush. I am at ease with you as I have not

* "A Bit of Blue" was the title of one of my pictures in the Royal Academy of the same year.

been with any one since I lost my own very dearest relations, and I am not the least afraid but that I shall tell you so again more earnestly next Christmas, if we all live. I can only write you this tiny card to-night, with truest wishes that your kindly and modest life may be more and more brightened with daily love, and due and tranquil prosperity.—Ever your affectionate,   J. RUSKIN."

These two charming and flattering letters are among the earliest I received. The correspondence continued for many years, interrupted only by the illness of my friend. Many of the letters, in fact most, I have preserved; some I regret to say are lost, for I had not then trained myself to those habits of order which I hope I have now, though there is still room for improvement. Some of these letters are undated, but as there is no need for chronological arrangement, this is less to be regretted. I shall content myself with giving whole or part of the more interesting or characteristic of them, with as few words of my own as are necessary for explanation.

Here is a reference to an evening spent at Hamilton Terrace, when Ruskin gave me a small daintily carved crane of opal :—

" DEAR MARCO,—We had a jolly night of it, of

which quite the brightest point to me was your
being so pleased with the little blue crane. I send
you a rough piece of the rock it came out of,
containing various illustrative pieces of colour. It
may lie about in your studio wherever you like, being
perfectly uninjurable, except by actual hammer-
stroke (it could only be scratched by diamond or
ruby): only it must not be on the chimney-piece,
or otherwise near fire, nor in hot sun ; all heat
above a certain point diminishness opal colour."

I sent Ruskin some bird sketches made from
life at the Zoo. He wrote from Corpus Christi
College acknowledging their arrival in these complimentary terms :—" I jumped all about the room
when I got your letter. I've been gloating like
a good vulture over those vultures ever since I got
them, and have got wilder and wilder about them
every day ; and I'm just going to show them in
my lecture here on Tuesday as examples of true
natural history drawing ; and all you tell me of
your feelings about them, and your work, at least
the issue of it in the Bird-room at the Duke of
Westminster's, is wholly delightful to me ; and that's
all I can say to-day, for I've been interrupted and
all my forenoon's gone."

A few days later I sent a batch of sketches by
book-post and rolled up, without any protecting

cardboard. By return of post I got the following remonstrance mingled with panegyric :—

" C. C. COLL., OXFORD.

" MY DEAR MARCO,—How I am ever to say enough or pay enough for those most precious drawings, I don't know, even if there's a letter with them, for I'm going to lecture upon them on Tuesday, and mean to open my lecture by show- ing the carelessness of a really great painter about his work, unfolding the parcel and investigating its crushed contents as I speak.

" I've only peeped in without unfolding, just to see how beautiful they are, and when I think of the impression they will make in being unfolded, I can't scold you for sending them so, as much as you deserve.

" I think this will begin an entirely new system of things in the Oxford Museum. Can't write more to-night. Ever your grateful,   J. R."

Across the top of this letter was written a post- script :—" Note found, after writing this, in a heap of unopened letters. Book-post indeed !"

On the same subject :—

" OXFORD, December 1877.

" MY DEAR MARCO,—I've just been framing the black crane with the red eyes with Turner and

Bewick, and he holds his own against both,—a glorious fellow! But look here! you must come and see it between the 5th and the 10th; all will be lonely, quiet, and you can see the Millais portrait and everything in the perfectest peace. We'll talk it over on Saturday when we meet at half-past two, and will have a time of it at Hengler's and afterwards. Arthur has arranged it all." . . .

And a merry party we made at an afternoon performance at Hengler's. Ruskin, Mr. and Mrs. Arthur Severn, my wife, two daughters, and self dining and finishing the evening at Hamilton Terrace. Soon after a brief visit to Ruskin at his rooms in Corpus Christi College was settled. Having specified the day and the train I thought most convenient to both, I had this brief but prettily expressed note in reply :—

"I must just say that that's the very nicest and best train you could possibly come by, and that all the birds are dying to see you, and I living more than usual for the same cause."

A very short but charming and interesting time I had at Oxford. I was there but two days, but saw and enjoyed a good deal in the time. We went to Dr. Acland's, in whose possession was the Millais portrait of Ruskin standing by a waterfall, of which I had heard so much and had long wanted to see. Ruskin showed me no end of his own treasures — the priceless drawings by Turner, the illuminated missals, the manuscripts of Walter Scott, of which that of "Woodstock" had special interest, knowing as I did the circumstances under which it was written, and the (to me) inconceivably short time in which Scott wrote it. The collections

of minerals, to speak frankly, had little interest for me, as I had no knowledge of mineralogy, and naturally, therefore, no power of appreciation. And the walks in the beautiful city, so rich in mediæval and academic architecture. I came away having had a happy time, but too short to give more than a fine, but confused picture of towers, churches, quadrangles, vaulted halls, libraries, and paintings.

The sale of Mr. E. B. Jupp's library, comprising books illustrated by the Brothers Bewick, wood-blocks, tracings, and drawings by Thomas Bewick, which occupied three days in its dispersion, was about to take place, and Ruskin asked me to attend the sale and buy for him certain lots which he wished to possess. I was delighted to have such a commission, for he gave me *carte-blanche*, and for the first and only time in my life could imagine myself as a connoisseur of unlimited means, to whom money was no object. My instructions were as follows :—

"BRANTWOOD, *February* 1878.

"MY DEAR MARCO,—That is just what I want. I like to give Severn the pleasure of buying, and of course you are the man in the whole world to choose what is my taste in animal drawing.

"Don't go against Leslie. I should like him to have all he cares for. If there's anything you think I should like much, and he doesn't want much, then he, I am sure, won't go against me.

"*No* anxiety, please, *no* sense of responsibility; just buy, you and Leslie, as you would for yourselves; but with *carte-blanche*, for drawings in pencil by his own hands, which Leslie does not want.

"Buy *no rare editions, no fine bindings, no*

blocks; only drawings and any cheap going copies
of the 'Birds'!"

My purchases were made on the second day
of the sale and comprised thirty drawings in
pencil for the "History of British Birds" for forty-
three guineas. Two water-colour drawings of
birds the size of life (a starling and a shrike)
for thirteen guineas, and two water-colour drawings of birds the size of life (a merlin and a
quail). For this last there was what is called "a
keen competition." Somebody else, a gentleman
from Newcastle, I think (who had already bought
largely), wanted it and bid against me. Beginning
at a guinea or so, the drawings ran up to ten and
twenty guineas. Pause—we began again; the
price got up to forty. Another pause—my rival
bid slowly, and as if each bid that he made was
anything but a free-will offering. For each of
his bids I made one higher, with the rapidity of
thought and the precision of machinery. Calm in
the consciousness that I possessed unlimited coin
(although another's), I waited till my opponent had
got to the length of his tether and made his last
bid; it was capped immediately by my offer of
sixty guineas. "Sixty guineas," repeated the auc-
tioneer; the hammer was held in the air for a
moment, and down it came with the well-known

sharp tap, which gave me as jubilant a feeling as if
I had been victorious in a contest for a Reynolds
or Gainsborough of many thousands.

"I was *delighted* with my Bewick," Ruskin wrote
a few days afterwards.   "I hope Leslie and you
had nice ones too."

The following refers to the birds I painted for
one of the drawing-rooms at Eaton :—

"*November* 1879.

"MY DEAR MARCO,—I've not been myself, and
couldn't get what I wanted to say of the birds,
into any clearness for you, but I must, at least,
say how entirely glad I am to see the strength
of a good painter set upon natural history, and
this intense fact and abstract of animal character
used as a principal element in decoration.   The
effort is so unexampled, that you cannot hope to
satisfy yourself, or satisfy all conditions of success
at the first trial.   But you have, at all events, done,
and the Duke is happy more than any patron
of art in these times, in having induced you to do
what will be the beginning of a most noble and
vital school of natural history, and useful, no less
than charming art.   I think you will have ultimately
to keep the foliage darker and flatter—and for my
own share *I* should like some blue sky and flying
birdies behind.   But I'm such a lover of blue

(except in beards, stockings, and devils), that I'm
no safe counsellor.—Ever yours, &c."

Here is an extract which I can transcribe un-
troubled by those blushes caused by others more
flattering.   What "the woful little sentence about
the humour" was in my letter to which this is
an answer, I have utterly forgotten, and am in
as equal ignorance as the reader :—

". . . And I had indeed a thrill and pang of remorse when I came to your woful little sentence
about the humour.   It is nevertheless too true, and
indeed some very considerable part of the higher
painter's gift in you is handicapped by that particular faculty, which nevertheless, being manifestly
an essential and inherent part of you, cannot itself
be too earnestly developed : but only in harmony
with the rest to the forcible point.   When you say
you are not a colourist, it merely means that you
have not cared to be one.—You have a perfect eye
for colour, but practically have despised it—just as
I despised my Father's taste for sherry, and now,
to my shame, don't know it from brandy and
water ! but that is simply because I never set
myself to watch the tongue sensations.   Colour
is to be learned just as Greek is learned, by
reading the best Greek masters ; and if we go

on colouring and talking Greek out of our heads
—however good the heads may be—they never
make headway.   When you painted your Convocation, you enjoyed the humour of the birds,
but not their likeness to the cloud and the snow
in relation to earth and sea—and I am certain
there is more strength in you, by a full third, than
you have yet discovered.—But it will only come
out if you put yourself under Tintoret's eagles
and Carpaccio's parrots, as well as under the wild
creatures themselves; just as Tintoret and Carpaccio learned of Jove's eagle his thunder—and of
Juno's peacock his eyes—and of Cytheræa's doves
her breath.   Nature never tells her secrets but
through the lips of a Father or a Master; and the
Father and the Master can say nothing wise but
as Her interpreter. . . . Believe me, &c.,

"JOHN RUSKIN."

The next letter is in the scolding mood, to my
mind very characteristic in its Ruskinian humour.
"Leslie's book" is his "Our River," published
in 1881.

"BRANTWOOD, *June* 5, 1881.

"MY DEAR MARCO,—I've written seven letters
to-day, after my own too hard work, all to people
who really need to be comforted, or scolded.   I've
little comfort in me and too much crossness, but

forgive me when I say that Leslie's book, sweet and honest as it is, has given me a worse notion than I ever had before of the elements of artists' life in London. You associate only with each other, and you want each to be at the top of the tree—when the top of it is far in the clouds above without any possibility of sight from that Thames level.—How many posts has Leslie drawn in that book altogether? Are they the souls of deaf Londoners?

"Good heavens! if you and he, and a few of your girlies and laddies, would only put on hobnailed shoes and start on a walking tour of France and the Tyrol, and see what life means—and the earth, and the sea—and tweak the picture-dealers' noses the first thing whenever you come into a town!—and I could get a glimpse of you en route. You never attend to what I say, of course, so good-bye.—Ever, &c. &c.,   J. R."

In a letter chiefly of a private and personal nature, I find a delightful bit about the Japanese treatment of birds, which should not be lost. The signature, "Conundrum," was owing to my having once called Ruskin "a conundrumical professor," on one occasion, when I could not reconcile two of his statements that appeared contradictory, or as I actually put it, "a man knows not when to have you":—

"I've been buying Japanese books of birds myself, but only to study their way of extracting the ugliness of things with vicious variety, and the way they gloat over black as if it was blue and gold! There's a 'peacock' in my book which looks like a cabful of old straw tucked through a broken gridiron!—Ever your affectionate,
"CONUNDRUM."

Here is a pretty glimpse of spring, with some hints and admonitions about bird-painting :—

"*April* 16, 1887.

"MY DEAR MARCO,—My little bantam came to crow at my window yesterday, to say it was spring, and the lambs were very eager to give me the same information. I hope it is spring for you also, but mind, you can't paint a bantam yet! don't go on drawing claws—or comic penguins. Try if you can paint a pheasant's head or a peacock's real size.— Your uncle,   JOHN."

I once sent Ruskin a water-colour drawing of an Adjutant Stork, either as a birthday or Xmas card. It was thoughtless of me—I might have known that he would not care for a creature so quiet in colour, and with less beauty than quaint grotesqueness of form. But I did not altogether regret having sent it, as I got such an individual

letter as that given below. The Adjutant was
returned with it :—

No date.

"MY DEAR MARCO,—Alas, the reason I have not

yet written about the adjutant was—it *must* out—
that I didn't like him : and that he gave me a
sorrowful impression of your being out of sorts, and
thwarted, not to say perverted in your work by

fog. London association of sight and sound—and—
Dukes and Academies. If you could take a little
cottage at Coniston with Mama and the girls,
and paint every one of our birds, from the blue tit
to the windhover, as you saw them, and with no
reference to decoration, to the line, or the newspaper, you would do lovely things—but at present,
you are literally walled up, every way.

" My main fault with the adjutant is that his bald
head makes me feel every time I look at him, if
I've any hair left on my own—next, that he isn't in
sunshine, casting no shadow to speak of, and yet
that his local colours don't come fresh and clean,
and his whole breast is rounded with grey *towards*
the light, till it actually comes dark against the
wall! while the wall itself is neither brick, stone,
nor honest plaster. And I am *amazedly* certain
that you are not making literally true studies from
natural chiaroscuro enough to keep your eye right.
I am sadly tired just now, and can only say in this
brutal way, what the facts are to my notion—but
I'm not a brute, but ever your affectionate uncle,

" JOHN."

In a letter which I have unfortunately lost,
Ruskin had again recommended a continental trip,
or rather a stay of some months abroad, with my
wife and daughters. However delightful the pro-

ject, it was simply out of the question. I had been at heavy expenses, buying the lease of and moving into another house, and was only just beginning to recover from them. I took the letter too seriously, and, on the impulse of the moment, must have answered it in a like spirit, for it produced this friendly expostulation :—

"BRANTWOOD, *June* 13, 1881.

"MY DEAR MARCO,—It is a punishment to me for writing too much in attempt, at least, to be sarcastic against my enemies, that my best friends think I can be sarcastic against *them*.

"But *you* with your splendid sense of humour, ought to have known, it seems to me, my earnest from my sneer, and least of all should you have thought that I could be sarcastic on poverty of *any* kind, how much less on a friend's, meritorious and beautiful in its every possible way—except only—living in London!

"Also, when I say 'I am cross' to any of my friends, it always means for their own sake, much more than for mine.

"In this matter, I may be cross with Leslie, for never honouring me during my ten years' work at Oxford, with a visit to my schools. And for you, my dear Marks, have not I at least these *ten* times asked you for sketches for my schools? You

choose to work for Dukes and Dealers, and I say
D. D. *both*.

"And that's all I can say 'to-day,' but it's for
your sake, not mine, though you mayn't think it.
I'll explain more afterwards.—From your uncle,

"JOHN."

In the last letter I have, dated from Brantwood,
in July 1883, there is this reference to a long
talked of visit together to the "Zoo":—

"It is a great joy to me that the Zoo will be
so happily possible.   All the news you give me
of the gardens, and all the messages from the
beasts delight my heart, and I have a number
of my bird-studies just waiting till I've seen the
guillemots under water."

The long talked of visit came off at length.
If I remember rightly, Ruskin slept at Hamilton
Terrace, and on the morning of next day, which
was Sunday, his brougham came from Herne Hill
to take us to the Zoo.   Dull and grey was the
weather, not a speck of his favourite blue was to
be seen in the sky—it was a raw rheumatic day,
in which the gardens looked gloomily.   If there
is a place that needs sunshine and brightness of
atmosphere for enjoying it thoroughly, that place
is the Zoo.   Having reached the principal entrance,
we went straight to the superintendent's office to

fetch the ever-courteous and obliging Mr. Bartlett,
and accompanied by him walked through the
gardens.   The new reptile-house had not long

been completed.   Mr. Bartlett, to whom was due
the conception and direction of all the internal
arrangements and contrivances for the safety of

the keepers while cleaning out the cases, feeding
the creatures, &c. &c., wished, with harmless pride
in the ingenuity of these contrivances, to point them
out to Ruskin and have his opinion of them. But
Ruskin caring for none of these things, turned a
deaf ear, began asking about poisonous lizards,
whether there were any such, if they had flat
triangular heads, where was their habitat, and so
on. I regret I made no notes of this visit or of
the conversation. The reptile-house was very quiet,
being the antithesis of the parrot-house, where all
is noise, movement, and brilliant colour. Here
all was silence, broken only by our voices and
the sound of our footsteps. In front of one case
I noticed Mr. Briton Riviere making notes of a
poisonous snake ; he was the only visitor present
besides ourselves. Thence we went to the fish-
house and watched the guillemots and penguins
swimming with marvellous rapidity as they gulped
their fish dinner with a celerity that augured well
for their digestive powers. As we strolled the
gardens in the misty air, Ruskin sought to understand from Mr. Bartlett how a bird begins its
flight—what mechanism of muscle it employs to
put its wings in movement, but his queries were
too subtle for the superintendent, who was unable
to satisfy his thirst for information. Bidding adieu
presently to our guide, we drove away, not without

an impression on my part that our visit had not been the success I anticipated.   Ruskin complained that the birds were always moulting, the beasts and snakes always shedding their coats.   All was imperfection—vanity and vexation of spirit.   The damp air, the grey colourless sky depressed us, and were responsible in a great measure for making the morning one of disappointment.

LARK.

CHAPTER XXIV

WHETHER the dog or the horse is the more popular animal in this country, is a question which I have not definitely settled in my mind, but I fancy if a poll were taken, the majority of votes would be in favour of the dog. There are thousands of people who know nothing of a horse,—or little more than which is the head, and which the tail end of that noble quadruped, whereas every one, if he does not keep a dog himself, knows a friend who does—and thus has opportunities of worshipping the creature and basking in the sunshine of his presence. The horse has been overrated, but not nearly to the same extent as the dog, to which animal he is far superior. His faults and shortcomings are mostly the result of the inhuman treatment of the men who attend on him, sometimes ignorant and neglectful, but oftener cowardly brutes with a fiendish ingenuity in

189

inflicting torture. The horse is docile and affectionate ; his temper, when bad, is the result rather of
nervousness, and the treatment he gets from
grooms and stablemen. Kindly, simple by nature,
he craves attachment ; if his sympathies are not
raised by human means, he makes friends with
some inferior being—with the harmless necessary
cat, with a lamb or goat, or even a bird. In the
stables of an hotel at Tiverton, there was a Cornish
chough, the companion of the horses. He was
a quaint, lively bird, who would call the landlady
of a morning, tapping at her door, and calling
" Mother, mother !" till she admitted him to her
room. His love of horses was the cause of his
death. Some strange horses were put in his
particular stable one day. The bird in misplaced
confidence approached too near to the heels of
one of them, who, startled by the unaccustomed
rustling, inadvertently kicked out and killed the
poor chough.

Those who have had a favourite horse, and
treated him uniformly with kindness and consideration, say he is a more intellectual animal
than is usually supposed. With such owners, little,
if any touch of the whip or spur is needed, and
the bridle is little more than a form, as the animal
can be directed by the touch of a finger, or tone of
a voice. The burly drayman of town, the leaner

ploughman of the country control their teams by word of mouth in a language of their own, understood only by themselves and the horses they drive. I seldom miss going once a year to the Military Tournament at the Agricultural Hall, Islington. It is one of the most interesting and wonderful sights I know of, as showing perfection of training in man and beast. I marvel still at the wonderful feats of the horses in a first-rate circus, and hope no cruelty is employed in the education of the animals. There might be less use of the bearing-rein with these, as with the carriage-horses of "the nobility and gentry," which are doomed to stand for hours, with strained and weary necks ; but reams of letters written to the *Times* have no effect, nor can kill a fashion, however ridiculous. The horse must above all things have a smart and "showy" appearance, though at the expense of his comfort or utility. In early days we read of the intelligence of the horse in Scott's novels—how the knight riding in the trackless forest, and having lost his way, threw the reins on the neck of his jaded steed, when the generous animal, responding at once to the trust put in him, pricked up his ears, mended his pace, and quickly reached the desired castle, thus modestly showing that his topographical knowledge was superior to that of his master. Many modern instances of this faculty testify to its truth.

We are told on the highest authority that "the
horse is a vain thing for safety," and it must be
confessed that, whether as a means of locomotion,
of losing your own money, or of winning that
belonging to other people, he is more or less un-
trustworthy.   How many have met their deaths
in riding their favourite animal?   What numbers
of the great, the good, and noble have perished
by the innocent heedlessness of the horse.   One
steps on a molehill, and straightway a king is dead,
leaving his sorrowing subjects in profound and
inconsolable grief; another stumbles on broken
ground, and an eminent pillar of the church has
fallen ; a third trips up on a smooth road, and we
have to deplore the loss of a brilliant orator and
sagacious statesman.   The list might be extended
indefinitely, but it is needless to arouse further recollections which cannot be otherwise than painful.

About winning or losing money on a horse I have
little to say, for the very good reason that I know
nothing about betting—have not the faintest idea
of what is meant by "starting prices" or "the
odds," and never made a bet in my life.   I have
not been on a racecourse, at least on the days
devoted to "the sport for kings," more than half-
a-dozen times, and on four of those occasions was
either taken by friends or accompanied them at
their earnest solicitation.   It was at Reading races

that a friend of mine, a landscapist, then a promising
man, since a celebrated painter, dropped several sovereigns over "the three-card trick," when I felt the
truth of the maxim attributed to La Rochefoucauld,
though doubtless uttered by scores of persons before
he was born—" That there is something in the mis-
fortunes of our friends that is not unpleasing to us."
At Lewes I saw a race run in a heavy thunder-
storm. It was grand to watch the black clouds
rolling over the downs; vivid lightning flashed,
torrents of rain fell and drenched the honest man
and the book-maker alike; the dingy hide of the
welsher had not been so well washed for months—
possibly for years. The hoarse shouts and yells of
the betting fraternity made themselves heard even
above the noise of the thunder. Just before the
conclusion of the race the storm cleared off—the
rain ceased, and a ray of warm sunshine lit up the
faces of the crowd with an orange light, relieved
strongly against the dark grey clouds. The yells
became louder as the horses neared the winning-post
—the perspiring, seething, coarse-featured, shape-
less-mouthed crew shouted their jargon until the
post was passed, when comparative quiet reigned.
It was a most impressive scene, as the gigantic
storm-clouds passed away with infinite variety and
play of light and shade over the distant downs: a
magnificent background to the mean, vulgar, and

debased humans. Nature delights in contrasts—
here she showed herself at once in one of her
grandest and meanest moods.

I have often wondered why so many men having
to do with horses should become degraded by the
association. The horse is not of a vicious nature,
why then should those who tend him become coarse
and brutal? I am not speaking of jockeys, grooms,
or stable-boys, though no doubt they have sins
enough of their own to answer for; but rather of
a body with whom I cannot help coming into un-
willing contact in walking up to town by the
Edgware Road. True, I might go by another
route, but that broad thoroughfare is for many
reasons more convenient. In one part of it is an
auction yard for the sale of horses, harness, and cabs
on two days of the week, a place like Aldridge's
in St. Martin's Lane, but smaller. Around the
gateway and stretching across the pavement, on
these days is a crowd of beings in the shape of
men, but with the aspect of brutes. They are
of the lowest type of horse-dealer—"horse-copers,"
I believe they are called, though I cannot find
the term in any dictionary I have. With these
there are many underlings to swell their numbers, horse-cleaners, stable-helps, and hangers-on
of every description, with an unlimited capacity
for drinks and strong language. All affect those

tight trousers which, if difficult to get on, must be still more difficult to take off. In their hands they carry whips or sticks, in their mouths, pipes or "twopenny smokes," offensive to the nose as they are to the eyes; they obstruct the traffic and offend the ears by their villainous and disgusting language. None can help hearing it, it has to be endured by women and children as well as by men. The police, I suppose, are powerless to enforce that fiction of the law which forbids obscene language in the public streets. But enough of these blackguards, the Yahoos of our race, with their loathsome habits and foul filthy talk.

The life of a horse, when not working, can, under the most favourable conditions, scarcely be regarded enviable as that of other domestic animals. Shut up in a stable for so many hours even with companions, or a favourite cat, however conducive to reflection, must be monotonous. Solitude, though delightful, may fail to display its charms to the horse as it did to Selkirk. The recollection of his past life, however blameless, can afford little variety of subjects for contemplation. Journeys long or short, loads more or less heavy to drag, the kindness of one master, the indifference of another, is there much more than these on which to exercise his memory? He would gladly ex-

change these reflections for an hour's scamper in
the neighbouring meadow, free and unfettered as
the wind. Can, or does the horse ever think
of the future in store for him? The future—
I have sometimes ventured to speculate, when
I see the sadly overworked horses—the patient
toilers of the omnibus, the wretched broken-
kneed screws of the night cab, the pariahs, the
outcasts of the horses of our large cities —
whether there is or is not a future state for the
hapless creatures who devote their weary lives
to our business or pleasure, and die worn out
in our service. Does the life of the horse end
with the pole-axe and the knacker's yard? Is
there no recompense or reward for him hereafter?
He gets none here. If there is a future state
for the tyrant, shall it be denied to the slave?
I put this hypothesis with tremulous diffidence,
as a plain unlearned man. Doubtless it may
have been thought out before. Yet it is a problem not unworthy the consideration of a bench
of bishops, though too trivial for the deliberation
of that assemblage of pugilists and politicians,
known as "the collective wisdom of the nation,"
which sits at Westminster, and talks so much and
does so little.

I am about to make a confession which will lower

me in the estimation of nine-tenths of those
who may happen to read these lines—a confession so heterodox, so profane, not to say
impious, that, in making it, I may perhaps alienate
the affection of some of my friends.   For some
time I debated whether this confession should be
made, whether it would not be better for my comfort and peace of mind, to conceal the sentiments
I am about to utter, in the depths of my inner
consciousness, than reveal them to an unsympa-
thetic world, and thus become an object of scorn,
but I find it impossible to conceal my thoughts,
so, regardless of consequences, I screw my courage
to the sticking-place, and boldly proclaim the incredible and fearful fact, that I dislike the animal
known as the dog, nay, regard him with feelings
even of loathing and detestation.   I have the less
hesitation in owning to such blasphemous views,
because hitherto the dog has had it all his own
way, and every kind of eulogy and adulation been
lavishly showered upon him.   Writers in verse and
prose have vied with each other in celebrating his
praise ; painters, not to be behind the poets, have
endowed him with expression more than human in
intelligence, as he watches at a rat-hole, or indulges
in various idiotic antics ; no pictures are so popular,
or find readier sale, than those which depict the
so-called friend of man, as a hero or a humorist.

Not only are pictures painted, but songs are composed for his glorification. Had he any sense of humility, the dog would blush at the fulsome flattery that has been heaped upon him, but his inordinate conceit has been petted and praised to such an extent, that he takes all, as scarcely his due, but rather as a feeble tribute to his overwhelming merit. There are two lines by Prior (slightly altered), which teach us how we should behave to the dog—

> " Be to his virtues very kind,
>   And to his faults be wholly blind."

Byron went so far as to belaud his favourite Newfoundland, at the expense of man, as some critics cannot praise a painter or author, without first depreciating every one else who has ever painted or written. The great poet's circle of friends, did we not know to the contrary, must have been very limited, to judge from the concluding lines of the epitaph, which he wrote for the tombstone of his dog—

> " To mark a friend's remains, these stones arise,
>   I never knew but one, and here he lies."

This epitaph must, I fancy, have been written after breakfasting on biscuits and soda-water, when the noble bard's liver was somewhat out of order.

If my remarks appear somewhat sweeping, I may remind the reader that there are dogs, and dogs—useful dogs and useless dogs. For the dog who pursues an honest occupation, and earns his own living, I have a respect that almost amounts to esteem, as the sheep dog, for instance, and, though I have little sympathy with what is known as "sport," can tolerate and even admire the intelligence of dogs trained for hunting or shooting purposes, when they accompany their masters on their killing or maiming expeditions. But the London house-dog, the creature who barks or howls continuously, and without cause— the noisy wretch who destroys the calm of a summer evening, and makes it all but impossible to sit in the open air by reason of his fiendish yelping or yapping—what can I say of him, but that he excites in me sentiments of aversion and disgust? I cannot even cough or sneeze in my own suburban garden, without exciting a fussy, inconsiderate demon to bark in another. What sarcasm to call such nuisances "dumb brutes!"—would that they were! In the streets the dog is still more objectionable; not only have you to endure his noise, you are liable to be attacked by him. So vain and self-conscious is the dog of the house that he cannot be let out for an airing without proclaiming the fact to all the neighbourhood for

a mile round; and should you be unlucky enough
to pass the house at the moment the beast is
issuing from the front door, he will, in the joy
and excitement of temporary freedom, rush at
you with open jaws and endeavour to leave a
proof impression of his teeth in the fleshiest part
of your leg. A young friend of mine, a doctor,
going on an errand of mercy, was once assaulted
in this way, when the playful animal tore a piece
of considerable size from his trousers, which happened to be a new pair. He remonstrated with
the owner of the brute, as she stood by the
street door, who, like a true woman, despite the
evidence of the torn garments, persisted in assur-
ing the young medico that her dog was harmless
as a kitten! " He won't hurt you," is the invariable
saying of the owner of the animal who flies towards
you in an aggressive manner. It is curious, but
no one ever owns a dog that is not of the most
lamb-like nature, and combines the wisdom of the
serpent with the harmlessness of the dove. Who
does keep or confess to keeping a savage dog?
Are there none in existence? In police court
cases it is always the same old story. The man
who doesn't love dogs, and has been annoyed or
injured by one, is in the wrong, while the owner
is ready to perjure himself by protesting that his
animal is perfectly innocuous. In too many cases

the doggist is a selfish being, into whose head never enters the idea that his neighbours are not dogolaters, and dislike the doggish noise and habits which afford him pleasure.

A dog kept in a large town, where he has too much food and too little exercise, is a mistake. In the country he is endurable, though whether, as Scott affirmed, he makes a pleasing object in the foreground, as you take your walks abroad, must always remain a matter of taste. Personally I prefer his room to his company. The dog's questionable manners and customs when taking exercise, whether meeting his friends or entire strangers, I will not do more than refer to. Having no ideas of his own to communicate, he will, as frequently as he can, interrupt the conversation of your friend and yourself. As you walk in company with a man of varied information and general intelligence, except in believing that he keeps a dog, when it is patent to all unprejudiced minds that the dog keeps him and makes him his slave,—as you walk, I say, with such a companion, the flow of talk will be arrested, the point of a story lost, by the vagaries of the dog. He is nowhere to be seen, and has to be whistled for. Again and again is the whistling repeated. But not until even the slavish master's patience is nearly exhausted, does the obedient creature come bounding round the corner, his tongue lolling out and a laughing expression in his eyes. His triumph is complete—he has made master and friend await his pleasure, and afforded another instance of the subjugating power of the dog over man!

The dog is a sycophant, inordinately vain and inquisitive. How he will fawn on a stranger! especially if that stranger should happen to be munching biscuits. He will fawn even on me, with or without biscuits, and whine piteously if I don't look at and admire him. This does not say much for that instinctive knowledge of physiognomy said to be possessed by children and dogs, which enables them to recognise the friendliness or the reverse of those in whose company they happen to be. The dog's vanity is hardly to be wondered at, when we think through what ages of flunkeyish flattery his race has lived. No gathering of women round an infant can be more enthusiastic about its real or fancied charms, than a party of the superior sex praising the points of a puppy. The puppy will become a dog, the dog will grow old, but he shall not cease to hear his praises sounded in his presence, and epithets as endearing as those which men address to the object of their affections before marriage, and discontinue afterwards, will be his portion until the day of his death. The inquisitive curiosity of

the dog no one can have failed to notice. As
he walks along the street he will thrust his nose
into every cranny and aperture, will look down
every area with that look of super-canine intelligence he is so fond of assuming, and invade with
eagerness any yard, court, or garden, the gate
of which is open. These proceedings have been
supposed to have some connection with an un-
quenchable desire of discovering cats, but should
one suddenly appear, and nobody be looking at the
time, our impostor will instantly sneak off—without
uttering a bark to betray his retreat.

But of all canine atrocities, surely that known
as the toy or lap-dog is the most disgusting and
offensive. Fat, lazy, and petulant, it is repulsive
alike to sight, smell, and hearing—its body a
shapeless mass of animated offal, its breath suggestive of anything rather than "Sabean odours
from the spicy shore of Araby the blest," and its
bark little more than a hoarse, pinguescent wheeze.
Alas, that lovely woman should be chiefly answer-
able for these "vile, ill-favoured faults!"—but she
is so delightfully inconsequential. Whether it be
a pug-dog or a husband, it is her first duty, she
considers, to fatten the animal by giving him
plenty to eat and drink, and thus ensure his
highest happiness. I don't include all ladies in
this category, for I have known many who would

spoil any creature rather than a husband. When
I see one of these shapeless masses of fat flesh
caressing its mistress, a comely, perhaps a hand-
some woman, as she allows it to lick her hands
and arms, the sight is not a pleasurable one.
Ladies have told me that these unwieldy darlings
make capital watch-dogs in houses of modest size.
It was not for me to contradict, but I thought of
the shepherd who shouted "Wolf" so repeatedly
that no attention was attracted by his cries, when
the farce had been repeated several times. I
should have thought when a lap-dog is yapping
all night the ears of the inmates would become
so accustomed to the noise as to cease to notice
it. On the other hand, it may be said, as I was
so frequently told in the days of my childhood,
that no creature is so vile, so ugly, or so apparently worthless but what it has been created for
some wise end, and was more especially designed
for the use and benefit of man.

If I have been too hard on the dog, whether the
over-rated Newfoundland, the barking and con-
ceited cur or terrier, the treacherous collie, or the
lazy lap-dog, let me make him some amends by
recording a few instances of his wonderful sagacity.
We will begin with a story of a Newfoundland :—

"Mr. Croizier, who is employed at the Jockey
Club, was bathing in the River Marne at La

Varenne on Saturday, when a fine Newfoundland dog by which he was accompanied, fancying that his master was in danger of drowning, dashed into the water and seized Mr. Croizier by the neck, arms, and body, and so brought him unwillingly to the shore. The dog appeared to be much pleased with the exploit, but his master was, on the contrary, greatly vexed, as he had been bitten by his over anxious companion in several parts of his body."

If it be said that this needs verification, a similar objection may be raised against many other anecdotes of canine intelligence. The story appears in a newspaper cutting in my possession, and the fact of its having appeared in one of the usual organs of public information ought surely to be sufficient guarantee of its truth.

Another owner of a sagacious Newfoundland was really in danger of drowning when taking a swim. His faithful animal, who evidently had a sense of humour, dashed into the water, and quickly reached his master. Each time the master's head appeared above water, the dog playfully patted it under again, repeating the process until death intervened, when, there being no need for further exertions, he swam back triumphantly to the beach.

Here is a story of a pet dog for the accuracy of

which I can vouch. My friend W. Burges, A.R.A.,
was a dog lover and a victim to canine blandish-
ments. He had a toy Maltese, or Skye terrier,
by name " Binkie," for which he had so great
affection and veneration that he got an artist to
decorate one of his painted cabinets with portraits
of Binkie in profile, full face, and three-quarter—in
half length and in full length. Of the virtues of
fidelity, constancy, and courage, this little animal,
which resembled the cheap earthenware chimney
ornaments of a country cottage, possessed more
than the ordinary share. A friend called one
day, Burges took the dog in his arms and began
sounding its praises to the friend, who was of a
sceptical turn of mind. " Dear little Binkie, she
understands every word I say now ; you pretend
to beat me, and see if she won't fly at you !" It
required but little courage to withstand an assault,
if one were made, from a creature so diminutive.
The visitor did as he was told, when the sagacious
little pet bit—not the visitor, but Burges himself.

Every one has heard of the dog who, being hard
up, requested the loan of a shilling from another,
who was in a less impecunious condition ; but
the following tale, related by Sir Edwin Landseer,
shows a keener insight in financial operations,
and is an instance of sagacity very remarkable as
proving how very fine the line must be which

separates instinct from reason. A gentleman was
staying at the country house of a friend, an owner
of and confirmed believer in dogs. The two took
a walk one morning, accompanied by a very intelligent retriever. The conversation naturally
turned on dogs. Ladies seldom tire of talking of
their children, their cleverness and complaints, so
the doggist is never happier than when enumerat-
ing instances of the wonderful qualities and virtues
of the animal of which he is the proud possessor.
" Look ! " said the dog's master ; " here is a five-
pound note, I will place it in the bole of this tree,
the dog shall not see me hide it, and when we have
walked some distance, we'll send him for it, and
he shall bring it back all right." After some time,
the friends returned homewards by another route.
" Go, fetch it," cried the master, without specifying
even what it was the dog was expected to fetch ;
however, away he trotted. Arrived at the house,
the two awaited his return. Some time elapsed,
the incredulous one began inwardly to chuckle—
another half-hour passed, and still no dog. At
length he appeared, but where was the note ? The
sceptic was considering how far he could venture
to chaff the whole business without giving offence,
when his host, taking the dog's head in his hands,
opened his mouth and displayed five sovereigns
concealed beneath the tongue. The delay was thus

accounted for. The dog had found the note, gone to the banker's in the nearest town, and exchanged it for gold!

The following newspaper extract, headed "Story of a faithful dog," is an example not so much of sagacity as of endurance :—

"Our Vienna correspondent reports that the son of a Dresden magistrate named Händ fell while climbing the Schrankögel, and was killed on the spot. His dog, which accompanied him, watched for four days by the body, which was eventually found by some shepherds, owing to the dog's barking." In this narrative, so circumstantial in its statements, we are not told whether the dog barked as well as watched, for four days. If he did, he was not only the champion barkist, but must have been possessed of a throat and lungs of more than leather-like consistency.

If I have said anything about the dog or his friends that seems unkind, I am sorry for it. I only ask the enthusiastic caniolater to think that there are people to whom the dog is less a creature to be loved than loathed. If Napoleon carried his dislike of the mouse so far as to be terrified by it, a humble individual may be pardoned for objecting to the larger and noisier creature. "Love me, love my dog," is a most imbecile proverb. Why, if I like a man whose only

weakness is shown in allowing a dog to keep him
and annoy his neighbour, should he expect me to
share my affection for him with his four-footed fetich?
No, nothing can ever persuade me to admire the
dog, and though not a Jew, although often claimed
as one, I must, with all deference to the doggist,
still regard that animal as an "unclean" beast.

Think not I speak of the dog without personal
acquaintance with that creature. In a moment of
weakness, I gave my consent, at the entreaties of
my family, to allow one to share our home. Contrary to my expectations, I have outlived the dog,
instead of the dog's surviving me. She was a half-
bred dachshund, presented to us by a friend, whom,
so far as I know, I never injured in word, thought,
or deed. What ulterior motives he had in giving
this additional occupant, I have never been able to
detect, though I have my suspicion. We named
this quadruped " Rus," a contraction of Ruskin,
with his consent—at least, I never heard him object
to our thus taking his name in vain. The dog was
female in sex, and of a gentle, fatuous, common-
place character, like many human beings, whose
good-nature is owing rather to an inability to be
sarcastic or disagreeable than to inherent amiability
of disposition. Selfishness was her chief, I may say
only fault, beyond the usual manners and customs
inevitable in the race. For instance, she would

only be contented with the centre of the hearth rug, in front of a blazing fire. If I ventured to dispute her right to this spot by standing for a minute or so in the favourite attitude the honest Briton assumes when before his own fire, her tearful expression of martyrdom would have melted any heart less stony than my own. Her power of enduring heat was something remarkable. Resting her fore-paws on the low stone fender, she would blink at the roaring fire till the heat was enough to desiccate what little brain continual roastings had left her. I had thoughts of designing a light screen lined with tin to shield her from the draught which always plays around the floor of a room, and thus concentrate the caloric on her body ; but the idea was abandoned in deference to the feelings of the family. She would also resent being turned out of a cushioned chair (her sagacity led her always to select the softest and warmest) with the same air of injured innocence as when politely asked to move from the centre of the fire. By judicious, kindly treatment, we induced her to abandon indiscriminate barking, reserving that dulcet sound for frightening those pests in a garden—the cats. We like our own cats, but detest those of other people. For more than thirteen years, in spite of over-feeding and too little exercise, Rus lived with us in peace and harmony. She was taken for change of air and her usual autumnal holiday in 1892. Travelling in the guard's van, she caught a chill on her return, and came back to Hamilton Terrace but to die. After lingering a few days the end came. It was announced to me while at work one morning. As I gazed on the inanimate form, it was with difficulty I could repress the rising tear. She sleeps under the shadow of the mulberry tree. A simple stone marks the spot and records her name and the day of her death.

CHAPTER XXV

SONGS AND VERSES ON VARIOUS OCCASIONS

I HERE venture to give a few specimens of verse, written at wide intervals and various times. I never was in any sense a facile or prolific writer, whether of verse or prose, and seldom ventured to woo the Muse without I felt she was in a pliable and yielding mood. If after a few minutes I found words and ideas would not flow readily, I gave up the attempt and sought relaxation in other ways. Thus the number of my rhyming attempts is not large, though it might have been considerably extended, but that I was warned that many of my lines were too personal in character. Unconscious as I am of having written any "line which dying I would wish to blot," some friends hold a distinctly opposite opinion, and, with an ingenuity which under other conditions might be considered praiseworthy, find sentiments and assertions in my humble lines, which I thought amiable and harmless, endowed with power to wound the susceptibilities of others. What I in my simplicity considered harmless as a child's india-rubber ball, was, they assured me, a bomb stuffed full of deadly dynamite. The personages who have figured in some songs are now no more, and I would not willingly hurt the feelings of any kindly survivor. Here is a ballad which I can't think can give offence to any one. It was written in 1852, a time in which I was deep in "Percy's Reliques," and knew many an old English ballad by heart. It is more or less, barring its melancholy conclusion, a record of my own experience. I am afraid I did not regard the antique in the days of my youth with great veneration, being impressed more by the quaint picturesqueness of Gothic sculpture than by the repose and beauty of Greek. Here it is to speak for itself.

THE DOLEFULLE BALLAD OF ARTHUR SCUMBLE;
OR, THE YOUNG PROBATIONERE.

1852.

Now lythe and listen, students all,
I come before ye here
To tell the mischance that befell
A yonge probationere.

Merrye it was in Londonne streetes,
The daye was fair to see,
When sallied forth an artiste youth
To the Royal Academye.

Hys looke is proude, hys step is lighte,
A drawynge in hys hande,
And now before thatte gloomye doore
This artiste youth doth stande.

Full syne he ryngeth at ye bell,
A portere opes the doore;
"O laye this drawing," quoth the youth,
"The Council-menne before:

And oh as ever they wold thryve,
Let them my fate decide
As speedilie as erst they may."
The portere nought replyed.

A month has passed, now in the school
Yonge Arthur Scumble draws,
Although with grievous mislyking
Of the Academye—its Lawes.

The skeleton doth worry him,
"Th' Anatomical" also,
Though thys is all th' anatomy
The student needs to know.

And now to draw the "figure"
He eagerly begins,
Though in the workynge of it up
Commytynge many sinnes.

He damns hys chalkes, he blastes hys bread,
And curseth not a few ;
He wysheth Woodyngton were dead,
And Charleye Landseer too.

"To save me from this dread antique
Wolde I hadde some kynde friende ;
Oh wyll thys dreary finnickynge
Be never at an ende ? "

But end it doth—the drawynge's done,
He hopes that itte may please,
And prayes to thatte effect at night
Upon his thread-bare knees.

Tyme rolleth on—the Council sittes,
The drawynges it selectes,
And once againe receives the worste,
Again the beste rejectes !

Yonge Arthur hastes hys fate to know
As faste as he maye hye—
A ruthlesse crosse against hys name
Proclaims hys miserye !

"Now, Heaven confounde them, one and alle,"
In rage aloud he cries,
And imprecations loud bestows
On Academic eyes.

Hys barnacles he dashed to earth,
He madlye tore his haire,
Hys rage was so extravagaunt,
It made the portere stare ;

In disorder of
mynde and
bodye he fleeth
from the
Academie.

And muttering an awfulle oath,
Blacke passion in hys face,
Dysordered dresse, dyshevelled haire
He rushed hym from the place.

He commytcth
suicide.

Thatte nyghte a corpse was borne along
The Thames hys darksome streame :
The alerte police yt soon secure
By moonlyghte's fitfulle gleame ;

And as to fynde out some addresse
Hys pockettes now theye fumble,
The bull's-eye light displayes the face
Of lucklesse Arthur Scumble.

The ende.

Thus endes the lyfe of this yonge manne,
God sende hym eternal blysse,
And all who drawe from the antique
Of Heaven may they never misse !

Amen !

There is a wide gap between this and the next studio song I have preserved. The Exhibition of the Royal Academy in 1874 will be remembered for the very great success of Miss Elizabeth Thompson's (now Lady Butler) picture of the "Roll Call," a success immediate as it was great. Familiar as it must be to everybody by the prints in the publishers' windows, it needs no description here. The popularity of the work in question was undoubtedly owing, not to the almost unique honour of being removed from the Academy walls during the Exhibition, and forwarded for her Majesty's inspection, nor to the complimentary remarks made on it by the Prince of Wales and the Duke of Cambridge at the banquet. It was the *humanity* in the picture which went straight to the public heart. The artist had struck a chord of human sympathy which makes the whole world kin. Lady Butler may have—indeed has—painted pictures since which have been technically superior, but never one that appealed so directly to popular sentiment. The song was written shortly after the opening of the Exhibition, when the furore was at its height : the circumstances herein related are all correct, and the speech of the Duke of Cambridge accurately reported.

THE ROLL CALL ;

OR THE ROYAL ACADEMY EXHIBITION OF 1874.

To th' Academy of course you've been,
And, after jostling crowds between
And waiting long, no doubt have seen
    The picture by Miss Thompson.
The " Roll Call " is this picture's name,
By it she's sprung at once to fame,
And put all painters else to shame,
    Indeed she has, Miss Thompson.

When dining with the swell R.A.'s
The Prince of Wales in graceful phrase
Spoke very highly in the praise
    Of Miss Eliza Thompson.

The Duke of Cambridge then began
And said, "that as an army man,
A better work he'd ne'er seen than
        This picture by Miss Thompson.

"I cannot understand," said he,
"How a lady young of twenty-three
So well up in our life can be
        As is the young Miss Thompson."
"She's firmly grasped," he said, said he,
"The soldier's speciality,
And this it is that quite beats me,
        Bravo! for young Miss Thompson."

To our gracious Queen then for a day
The picture's sent by the R.A.;
The public frets while its away
        And shouts "Why, where's Miss Thompson?"
"Why can't the Queen come here?" they say;
"Why should she have the work away
When shillings we to see it pay?
        What honour for Miss Thompson!"

The controversies in the Press
Contribute to the great success,
And widely advertise, I guess,
        The picture of Miss Thompson.
To carping critics she replied,
Who the action of the horse decried,
But all their statements she denied,
        Right bravely did Miss Thompson!

Some writers on the opening day
Said that the title A.R.A.
Should be conferred without delay
    On talented Miss Thompson.
Through Queen, Prince, Press, and public she
Has supped quite full of flattery ;
Let's hope that not quite turned will be
    The head-piece of Miss Thompson.

Well, now I've little more to say,
Save that to hope next year in May,
When the " Roll " is called on opening day,
    In front will be Miss Thompson.
May she ne'er " Halt " * in her career
But " Gallop " * forward without fear,
And ne'er be " Missing " * any year,
    So fare you well, Miss Thompson.

Next in point of date was a commemoration of the election of three A.R.A.'s in January 1874, Messrs. Ouless, Stone, and Graham. It is noteworthy that of the ten painters enumerated by the " young Academician " as " likely men," all, with one exception, have become members of the Academy. In the fourth stanza allusion is made to a regulation which no longer exists. When the voting papers had been handed round, each member placed a mark or " scratch " against the name which he

---

* Titles of works exhibited previously at the Dudley Gallery by Miss Thompson.

fancied most in the list, signed his own name at
the foot, folded the paper, and placed it before
the President, who, when all the papers had been
handed in, read out in audible tones the marked
names in succession. Signing the paper was
abolished eventually, but years after. An unsigned
paper would be torn in half, thrown into the waste-
paper basket, and the vote it recorded became null
and void. I remember this incident occurring
once, and availed myself of it as a good point.
I had no particular "Academician," "old," or
"young," in my eye, but it is easy to divine the
individuality of one, at least, of the middle-aged
Associates. Mr. Layard in his "Life and Letters
of Charles Keene" gives an extract from a letter
of my old friend in which he refers to this ballad.
"I enclose for your scrap-book a *jeu d'esprit* by
my friend H. S. Marks, A.R.A., a parody on a
popular ballad. He sings it when there are no
R.A.'s present. He does not want it to appear
in print, so don't let any chiel take note of it."
Keene made a little mistake here. The first time
I sang it was at a dinner of the Academy Club
at Willis's Rooms, and have since often sung it in
the presence of R.A.'s, but they took it in good
part and without anger.

ELECTION OF A.R.A., JANUARY 1877.

AIR—"*The Two Obadiahs.*"

Said a young Academician to an old Academician,
   "An election, sir, is coming on to-night."
Said the old Academician to the young Academician,
   "That fact I had forgotten—almost quite ;
But sorry I should be were I absent from the fray,
   So when I've wrapped up warmly we'll be off to the R.A. ;
And we'll take a cab together, for which I will let you pay."
   Said the young Academician, "I am on!"

In the Cab.

Said the old Academician to the young Academician,
   "Can you tell me now about the likely men ? "
Said the young Academician to the old Academician,
   " I should think there must at least be eight or ten.
There's Fildes, J. Archer, Holl, Riviere, John Brett, and
         Marcus Stone,
   Peter Graham, Morris, Prinsep, all of them well known :
Young Ouless, too, for portraiture some aptitude has shown."
   Said the old Academician, "So he has !"

Said the young Academician to the old Academician,
   " Let me whisper in your ear my little plan."
Said the old Academician to the young Academician,
   After cogitating deeply, " I'm your man !
But supposing on the Ballot now they should our man reject,
   May I ask, do you imagine, or should rather say expect,
With a sculptor they'll come over us, or else an architect? "
   Said the young Academician, " That be damned ! "

In the Assembly-Room.

Said the old Academician to the young Academician,
  " A very good assemblage here to-night."
Said the young Academician to the old Academician,
  " Let us hope, old man, the voting will go right."
The papers then were handed round to ev'ry man who came,
  But our ancient friend forgot to sign his highly honoured
    name.
  His vote was last, his paper torn, to his dismay and
    shame.
  The young Academician spoke of " eyes ! "

The Return Home.

Says the old Academician to the young Academician,
  " Well, I think, upon the whole, we may be glad."
Says the young Academician to the old Academician,
  " Yes, I told you Walter Ouless was the lad ;
  For he's not the boy to be puffed up by aught that people
    say,
  But he'll take his honours quietly, and you'll never see the
    day
  When he will shirk his work because we've made him
    A.R.A."
  Said the old Academician, " Dear, dear me ! "

Said the old Academician to the young Academician,
  " Now tell me what you think of Peter Graeme ? "
Said the young Academician to the old Academician,
  " That he wasn't ' in ' before's a burning shame !
  Though I wouldn't hint for worlds the Academy's not right,
  Yet Peter on the Ballot's been ten times before to-night.
  So I for one shake hands with him : he's made a gallant fight ! "
  Said the old Academician, " So I think."

Said the old Academician to the young Academician,
  " I should like to hear your views on Marcus Stone."
Said the young Academician to the old Academician,
  " That's another case of justice, all will own.
For seventeen years or thereabouts, on the line his work
     we've shown,
  Perspective, drawing, both correct, his colour good in tone:
So let's drink the healths of Ouless, Peter Graeme, and
     Marcus Stone."
  Says the old Academician, "We will drink!"

Moral.

There are old Academicians, there are young Academicians,
  There are middle-aged Associates as well;
But the old Academicians so much like their warm positions,
  That they never will retire—what a sell!
Yet we could mention one or two who've had an innings
     fair,
  Who now with grace might well vacate the Academic
     chair,
Then quickly with Associates their loss we might repair.
  Say the old Academicians, " Not so green!"

Here is a nursery rhyme on the first of the
successful trio :—

     There is a young painter named Ouless,
     Who to London came, ragged and shoeless ;
     Yet he'll make a rich marriage,
     And ride in his carriage,
     If he *will* only use Prussian-blue less.

Let me assure any matter-of-fact reader who,
with a limited sense of humour, is in the habit of

taking every assertion *au pied de la lettre*, that Mr. Ouless did *not* come to London ragged and shoeless, and is *not* in the habit of using Prussian-blue to an inordinate extent. The exigencies of rhyme must frequently dominate facts.

The two following may be called "dirges," as they relate to that depression from which Art, like Commerce, has been suffering of late. I have been told that such subjects are too sacred for jesting; that the revelations, if revelations they are, made in them, had better be concealed than written of. I confess I am unable to view the matter in this light. When it is matter of daily remark in the press that kings, emperors, nay, even nations are feeling the pangs of impecunious-ness; that every profession is over-crowded, and the difficulty becoming daily greater for the middle-classes to know what to do with their sons, and how to start them in life, why should the artist resent the fact being known that painting and sculpture are at a low ebb? I don't say my view is the right one, but cannot for the life of me see any harm in striving to extract a little fun from the situation. And I would again warn my matter-of-fact friend not to interpret too literally these lines, descriptive of a phase of the Arts which, after all, can be but temporary.

THE LATE LAMENTED PICTURE-BUYER.

AIR—*Obvious.*

Oh! where, and oh! where, is your picture-buyer gone?
Oh! where, and oh! where, is your picture-buyer gone?
I can't precisely say, but he's left me all forlorn,
And often I wonder, why was I a painter born?

Oh! tell me, pray tell, your late buyer's final fad?
Oh! tell me, pray tell, your late buyer's final fad?
He'd buy up Romney, Reynolds, and all dark "old
    Masters" bad;
His scorn for living British Art was really quite too sad!

Oh! where, and oh! where, did your picture-buyer dwell?
Oh! where, and oh! where, did your picture-buyer dwell?
In London, chiefly—Manchester—and all large towns as
    well—
Now sleeps he 'neath the mould, and we sadly toll his
    knell.

THE DAYS WHICH WE SOLD PICTURES IN.

STANZAS WRITTEN IN NOVEMBER FOG.

AIR—*Evident.*

I.

Oh, the days which we sold pictures in
    Are still to mem'ry dear,
Though they have vanished into space
    For many a weary year.

We ne'er shall see their like again,
    Nor prices get like those
With which the eager buyer would
    Incontinently close.
Now feel we hardness of the times,
    Our debts still daily grow ;
Ah, the days which we sold pictures in,
        A long time ago !

II.

We then were young and light of heart,
    No cares to drive away ;
And, oh, the joy to see one's work
    Well placed at the R.A.
The critics then were gentle, kind,
    And hailed " the rising man."
(As we grow old, 'tis sad to find
    How different's their plan.)
We next aspire to build a house,
    At least, a swell studiō ;
Ah, the days which we sold pictures in,
    A long time ago !

III.

The house is built, at Kensington,
    Or Sainted Wood of John,
And honours, ending in R.A.,
    Come quickly crowding on ;
The dealers flock around our doors,
    And all our work would buy ;
A few short years, and now 'tis known
    They've grown absurdly shy.

Both they and patrons soon will be
   Extinct as the Dodō;
Ah, the days which we sold pictures in,
   A long time ago!

IV.

Financial failures all around,
   With money scarce and tight,
The future seems to me, my friends,
   Extremely far from bright.
Now tens of thousands of young moths
   Are flutt'ring round the Art;
They'll burn their little wings, I fear,
   And feel, like us, the smart.
" Anch' io son pittore," then
   They won't so gladly crow;
Ah, the days which we sold pictures in,
   A long time ago!

V.

Too late to turn to other trades
   At fifty years or more,
While younger craft go sailing by,
   And leave us on the shore.
And should we try the "mackerel" game
   Upon the pavement hard,
Perhaps *that* line of Art's "full up,"
   And we from it debarred.
No refuge but the workhouse, then,
   "Remote, unfriended, slow;"
Ah, the days which we sold pictures in,
   A long time ago!

The songs and verses having any allusion to Art, however slight, end with the above. A couple of Christmas canticles, written with a view of promoting kindly feeling at the festive season, may be inserted here. That entitled "My Relations" seems severe, but is not serious. It is all in play. Written rather of other's relations than my own, I disclaim for it all charge of personality. The thoughts on Christmas morning embody perhaps the ideas of the average Paterfamilias more truly than the gush and sentiment which fill the Christmas numbers of various journals.

MY RELATIONS.

When an infant in arms, who was it predicted
The gallows would finish my earthly career,
Or at least a long lease of this life interdicted?
     My relations.

And who, when at school, were ne'er known to tire
Of saying my parts and my progress were small;
That the Thames would by me ne'er be set upon fire?
     My relations.

Who called it a false step in life when I married?
Who deemed me improvident, selfish, and vain,
And said that much longer I ought to have tarried?
     My relations.

With the method and plans for my child's education,
Who always would offer unasked-for advice,
And make me an idiot by kind implication?

My relations.

My efforts in literature, art, or the drama,
Who sneered at with praise so exceedingly faint,
As to cause me to mutter "Confound him!" or "D—n her!"

My relations.

And when on my death-bed I'm peacefully lying,
Who'll talk of, and hope for, "a speedy release,"
While surprised that I take such a long time in dying?

My relations.

Who, when under the turf I am finally resting,
As they gaily drive home, will discourse on my will,
And the sum for which I shall "cut up" be contesting?

My relations.

THOUGHTS AT CHURCH ON CHRISTMAS MORNING.

It is the holy Christmas-tide;
The parson works the well-worn trills,
And prattles much of love and peace,
But never mentions Christmas bills.

What though the weather's dark and drear,
The vile east wind your liver chills,
Let's gladly sing the Advent Hymn,
And wait the coming Christmas bills.

Replete with Christmas cheer, you take
Your Cockle's Antibilious Pills,
And penitently think upon
More drastic doses—Christmas bills.

Your little ones around you flock,
With "tuck" their tender tummies fill;
You call the doctor in next day,
Who adds another Christmas bill.

Your relatives, who all the year
Your kindly actions count as nil,
Will rally round your table now,
And help to swell the Christmas bill.

With trade depressed and money tight,
Bank balance low and empty tills,
'Twill try your Christian courage, friends,
To face and fight your Christmas bills.

For nearly nineteen hundred years
These words have caused ecstatic thrills:
"On earth let there be love and peace,
And unto men good Christmas bills!"

This chapter may conclude with the "Puzzled Parent and Precocious Child." The original of the latter was a little boy whom I had the pleasure to meet at a country-house. His countenance was "sicklied o'er with the pale cast of thought," and his frontal bone immensely developed. He was, perhaps, the most objectionable child I ever met. His stores of information were vast and varied. To say that he was an infantine ency-clopædia gives no idea of his fund of recondite knowledge. When he entered the room, I fled from it. If I failed to escape him, he at once attacked me, and quickly reduced me to a state of hopeless imbecility. There was no standing against him. He floored me with his vastly superior fund of information and left me without a leg to stand on. I was absolutely joyful when the time for my departure arrived. I never saw him again : his body was too fragile for such a soul. He died after an illness of moderate dura-tion, leaving a sorrowing father to mourn his loss—a loss sustained with an uncomplaining heroism as touching as it was unexampled.

THE PUZZLED PARENT AND THE PRECOCIOUS CHILD,

WHO DIED AT AN EARLY AGE.

"Oh, Daddy, lay your paper down,
    And talk with me a while ;
Don't, please, put on that serious frown,
    But let me see you smile.
Some things there are I can't make out
    While I'm awake at night,
Which in my mind oft cause the doubt
    What's wrong, and what is right.

So I will ask my dear old Dad
  Unto myself I said."
" Say on, my boy, but don't be long;
  It's nearly time for bed!"

" To Church, on Sunday, when I go,
  The preacher *Peace* proclaims;
Says we are Christians, and will show
  How virtuous all our aims.
But this I cannot understand—
  We send out men with guns
To rob poor heathens of their land
  And kill those dark-skinned ones,
Whose only crime appears to me
  That for that land they've bled."
" It's getting late; high time it is
  That you went up to bed."

" And why, in talking politics,
  Do men their tempers lose,
And constantly ' the other side '
  So angrily abuse ?
' Tories are fools,' cries Mr. Jones,
  ' The brains are with the Rads ;'
While Mr. Brown the Liberals
  Defines as ' awful cads.'
Now, this is surely childish, Dad,
  When all is done and said."
" Confound it all ! it's half-past eight ;
  You ought to be in bed!"

" They tell me God is kind and good
  He loves each bird and beast ;
To each in season gives its food,
  The largest as the least.

And yet, last winter, lambs and sheep
  Were frozen in the fold;
The fish in icy death did sleep,
  And birds were killed by cold;
'No sparrow falls without His will,'
  I've in my Bible read."
"Oh, hang it! Where is Jane? Oh, Jane!
  Pray, put this boy to bed!"

Specimens of some extinct buyers.—

17 HAMILTON TERRACE N·W·

H. STACY MARKS
AT HOME
day Evening
188
8 to 12

MORNING DRESS

MANY years ago, when I was but a youth, a song was going about the town that attained very great popularity. The words were simple and their air catching; each verse ended with the refrain—

" Every morn as true as the clock,
Somebody hears the postman's knock."

At the Haymarket Theatre on a benefit night, between two pieces, an actor dressed as a postman, with a bag on his shoulder and a bundle of letters in hand, sang this song with electrical effect, accompanied by the whole orchestra, one member of which executed the postman's knock at the proper intervals,

234

by means of some mechanical contrivance, with a realism that was startling by its accuracy.

How differently does the sound of the postman's knock affect members of a household! The younger ones, especially the girls, rush to the house-door if they expect anything "nice," and will be unusually punctual at the breakfast-table. Paterfamilias, on the other hand, is in no hurry. Long experience has taught him what to expect in multitudes of circulars for wine and coals, for the restoration of a church, for the enlargement of a hospital, or a testimonial to some busybody of whom he never heard, for performing some action of which he entirely disapproves. Benevolent individuals offer to lend him any amount of money, with or without security, while the needy make application for loans, which, individually not large in amount, would collectively require more than the largest known fortune to satisfy.

Compared with these communications, the letters of the common or garden autograph-hunter are less annoying. He always begins his application with the flattering assurance that he is making a collection of the handwritings of "the most distinguished painters of the day," and ends it by apologies for presuming to take up your "valuable time." When the autograph collector encloses a stamped and directed envelope, you oblige him with a specimen

of your penmanship; if he fails to do this, away
with his missive to the waste-paper basket. Sometimes a collector, instead of asking frankly for what
he wants, goes in a roundabout way to get it.
Thus a man once enclosed a carte-de-visite and
asked "if I thought it was intended for me?" I saw
through the dodge, and got one of my daughters to
answer for me :—" My father wishes me to write
that he thinks the photograph, which he now
returns, must have been intended for him, as he
remembers sitting for it some two years ago."

Everybody, I suppose, judging from my own experience, gets a certain number of what may be
called "silly letters." One's first impulse is to destroy these, but a second reading may alter this
resolve. I generally now keep them, and sometimes
answer them, and here offer a few samples. Here
is a specimen to which I could only reply in the
way I have :—

No. I.

(Copy.)

"DUBLIN, 1892.

"DEAR SIR,—Pardon my intrusion. May I ask
you to be so kind as to inform me which of your
works gave you the greatest pleasure, both in the
conception and working out of the subject.—Yours
sincerely."

(Reply.)

"1892.

"DEAR SIR,—In reply to your letter, I have to inform you that I am not clever at guessing conundrums, and am quite unable to answer yours.— Faithfully yours, H. S. M."

That was a hard nut to crack, but the following was a poser :—

No. II.

(Copy.)

"HAMMERSMITH, 1892.

"SIR,—I am compiling a book in which I wish to include the shortest definition of 'Pre-Raphaelitism.' Will you graciously contribute it ?

"A non-reply I shall loyally take as an intimation that I have attempted to trespass on your too valuable time.—I remain, &c."

I *did* reply to this, saying the writer appeared to be "compiling" a book by the ingenious method of getting others to write it for him, and though my time was not "too valuable," I had other ways of employing it.

The following from an Art student living in Birmingham requires no introduction :—

No. III.

(*Copy.*)

"BIRMINGHAM, *September* 1892.

"DEAR SIR,—As an Art student and anxiously seeking after knowledge, I was looking through a publication known as the 'Art at Home' series a short time ago, when I came across a notice to the effect that you were preparing a work on painting to be published in same. I should be most pleased to know if you have done so, as I am anxious to possess a copy. I am also anxious to know something of mediums, and anything appertaining to the art of figure-painting as applied to pictures. A reply would be considered an honour.—Yours very truly."

I thought it a little odd that an Art student living in so important a town as Birmingham, which, besides a Museum and Art Gallery, has ten or eleven Art schools, attended by some two thousand students, should experience any difficulty in getting the information referred to in the latter part of his letter. I replied as follows :—

(*Reply.*)

"*September* 1892.

"DEAR SIR,—There was some talk about my writing a volume for the 'Art at Home' series years ago, but the project fell through from various causes. There is a volume of the series entitled 'Sketching from Nature' by Mr. J. Tristram Ellis, which combines amusement with instruction.

"With regard to mediums, as an Art student you must go to some school; that school must have a master; that master is surely able to tell you what you require to know. But should he be unable to supply the requisite information, I would advise you to attend a spiritualistic séance where you will, with ordinary observation, learn enough about mediums to last you your life.—I am, faithfully yours, H. S. M."

The next specimen, also from a young man, is tolerably cool :—

No. IV.

(*Copy.*)

"CHELSEA, 1892.

"DEAR SIR,—Having been invited to contribute an article to *Cassells' Saturday Journal* on 'the Difficulties of Artistic Posing,' I should regard it as an honour and a favour if you would kindly inform me as to your own methods for placing your bird-models in the required attitudes. I should be obliged, also, if you would tell me how and where you obtained your early knowledge of anatomy. Any spicy little anecdote relating to your experiences at the Zoological Gardens and elsewhere would be very very acceptable.—I am, &c."

Here was an opportunity for a little chaff which I found it impossible to resist. The idea of "placing" a bird, of all creatures the most restless, was *too* comic, and I at once answered my correspondent in the following words :—

(Reply.)

"September 1892.

"DEAR SIR,—My methods for 'placing my bird models' are extremely simple. From frequent visits to the Zoo, many of the birds have learned to know me, and we have formed friendships which I trust 'death alone can sever.' Relying on these amicable relations, and knowing what perfect linguists they are, for all birds, more especially those of the parrot tribe, understand, if they do not speak, several languages besides their own, I have only to say, either in French, Spanish, or German, as the humour takes me, 'Will you kindly stand on one leg with wings outstretched—head a little more to the right, please—thank you—now steady!' when the sagacious creature will assume the required attitude and remain motionless for as long a time as I require for taking its portrait.

"My 'early knowledge of anatomy' must, I fancy,

have been imbibed simultaneously with the nourishment I received from my mother, for it is so long
ago that memory refuses to recall the date.

"As for 'spicy little anecdotes' connected with
my experiences at the Zoo, you will pardon me
if I retain them for my own use in case I should
ever write those experiences. I am not, I regret
to say, of so generous a nature as to give them
for 'copy' to one whose acquaintance I have not
had the honour of making.—Believe me, &c.,

"H. S. M."

The foregoing comprise the choicest gems of
silly letters relating to Art which I have preserved.
We now come to two circulars on more serious
subjects. It has happened to some men to read
their own obituaries while yet living and in the
best of health : to read the real impressions some
one had of them when alive, and can now record
with pleasant candour, thinking them dead. It
must be rather an ordeal for the subject of "our
obituary notice." Such a pleasure I have never
enjoyed ; but only a few weeks ago I received a
circular from a firm of cemetery marble and stone
masons, addressed to "the representatives of the
late H. S. Marks, Esq., M.A.,"—in which were a
number of lithographs of tombs, memorial crosses,
&c. I wrote to the firm this mild remonstrance :—

No. V.

(*Copy.*)

"*April* 1893.

" SIRS,—I am in receipt of your circular addressed
to the representatives of the late H. S. Marks, M.A.
I am not M.A., but R.A. ; am not late, but alive
and in good health.

" Doubtless you may, at some time in your lives,
have come across the verse 'where the carcase is,
there will the vultures be gathered together.'

"You have ingeniously given a new reading to
that verse, and shown how the vultures may be
gathered together without the excuse of a carcase
for their meeting.—Yours, &c.   H. S. M."

In this letter I took the liberty of substituting
"vultures" for "eagles," which stands in the received
version of Scripture. I don't know whether that
verse has been correctly translated, but vultures
were doubtless meant.   The eagle kills his prey
himself.   The vulture will eat what has been killed
by others, and is not particular if his meal be a
little "high."

But the letter which pleased me most was one
from a clergyman, who, thinking from my name
I must be a Jew, endeavoured to convert me by
means of certain services he was then conducting
for the benefit of the Israelitish people generally.

As the letter, or, to be strictly accurate, the lithographed circular, is somewhat lengthy, I have taken the liberty of slightly condensing it, but not otherwise altering it in any way.

No. VI.

(*Copy.*)

"*October* 1881.

"My dear Sir,—I have long had the children of Abraham on my heart, and wish I had more frequently personal intercourse with them, especially those of you who are my neighbours. I am persuaded that we Gentiles owe your fathers a deep debt of gratitude for preserving the books of the Old Testament with so much care, and handing them down to us. . . . May I therefore be permitted! to invite you to hear what we have to say on some of these grand topics, in addresses to be delivered in my church, &c., &c.—Believe me, &c., &c."

(*Reply.*)

"Dear Sir,—You are labouring under a mistake. I never had an ancestor named Abraham, so far as I know; but as I cannot trace my descent beyond my grandfather, this may account for my ignorance. I am what is called a Gentile or Christian, and have most of the vices of members of that persuasion. Had I been a Jew, I should have resented your attempt to convert me from a faith which can at least claim a greater antiquity than yours or mine.—Faithfully yours,   H. S. M."

To this letter I have never received a reply.

If the letter marked No. IV. is remarkable for coolness, the following excels it, and the writer must possess what in student days we were accustomed to call "a pretty tidy nerve :"—

No. VII.

(*Copy.*)

"*July* 1893.

"DEAR SIR,—I have the pleasure to inform you that I am shortly bringing out a very interesting and *high-class* work on 'Blankshire Men of Mark,' and in order that it may be more *complete*, I have just started preparing a complimentary sketch of you for the book.

"You shall see a proof for private *revision* in due course.

"Might I please to trouble you to send me at once your photo for the volume ?

"As the book, owing to the superior nature of all its details, is costing a very heavy sum to produce, I am confidentially asking the various noblemen and gentlemen appearing in it to kindly take twenty pounds' worth of copies each when the work is out.

"I presume you also will be agreeable to extend similar support to the interesting book, and needless to say I shall very highly appreciate your kindness.

"I am quite sure you will be delighted with the work when out. Please to forward photo promptly and oblige.—Yours, &c. &c."

(Reply.)

"July 1893.

"DEAR SIR,—In answer to your letter, allow me to say that 'sketches,' complimentary or otherwise, have long since failed to have any charm or interest for me. And permit me to add, that if you find noblemen or gentlemen willing to pay for twenty pounds' worth of your advertisement of them, another illustration will be afforded of the truth of that proverb which refers to the quickness with which certain people and their money may be parted.—Faithfully yours, H. S. M."

SKETCH BY G. DU MAURIER.

CHAPTER XXVII

BOOK-PLATES, OR "EX LIBRIS"

THERE are yet many persons who don't know what a book-plate is, and more who never heard of it by its singular equivalent *ex libris*. It has been defined as "a piece of paper stamped or engraved with a name or device pasted in a book to mark the ownership." Not so very many years ago the book-plate had no value commercially; at length the collector appeared, the demand gradually increased, and sent up prices. Stray references to the subject appeared in *Notes and Queries* and antiquarian magazines. The Honourable H. Warren wrote a guide to the study of book-plates, which was published in 1880, and is, I believe, out of print. Later, in 1892, an illustrated handbook for students of *ex libris* appeared, written by Mr. Egerton Castle,—a work which can be recommended as supplying all information on book-plates. About four years ago the Ex-libris Society was established, which is in a very flourishing condition, with over 300 members. It possesses

a journal, published once a month, which, besides
being a medium of intercommunication with the
members, gives the latest information on their
favourite study, and is illustrated by reproductions
of rare and interesting specimens. Collectors are
daily on the increase; those who started years ago
have amassed enormous numbers of plates, if I dare
venture to say so, more remarkable for quantity than
quality. Classified in styles, we have the Armorial,
the Chippendale, the Pictorial or Decorative, Book
Piles, Library Interiors, &c. I have looked through
many collections, and, generally speaking, found in
them more that appealed to the herald and genea-
logist than to the artist. Yet there are many admirable examples designed by the old men, to mention
only Albert Dürer, Holbein, and lesser artists
influenced by them; while to-day there is an
almost unlimited list of men capable of designing
beautiful and artistic work, who have proved their
capacity by the production of plates distinguished
by good drawing, invention, and fanciful feeling.
Of these I will only mention Erat Harrison,
Walter Crane, C. W. Sherborn, E. A. Abbey, and
John Leighton, though I could easily prolong the
list. But examples of those artists are comparatively rarely in the folios of collectors compared
with "Armorials," merely heraldic book-plates of
coats of arms and crests, commonplace in character,

without design, without taste, without feeling,—the common or garden book-plate, which is seen in the windows of seal-engravers or die-sinkers, and which has even less relation to art than the humble attempts of the individual who decorates the pavement of our streets. So when a man resolves on having a book-plate of his own, in nine cases out of ten he takes the aid of a tradesman rather than of an artist. There is much to be done in elevating the taste, as it appears to me, both of those who collect and those who commission book-plates. All is fish that comes to the collector's net, and so long as a specimen is scarce, the rarity of it will excuse any amount of ugliness or want of artistic skill. Pictures are an expensive luxury, to be indulged in by comparatively few, but a work of art in the form of a good book-plate, is attainable by all for a moderate sum. Let the *Ex-libris Journal* see to it, and cultivate a better taste, by giving a larger number of examples which have something more to recommend them than the piles of books defiant of the laws of perspective, or the ill-drawn armorial coats devoid of composition or decorative feeling, which we see so often in its pages. There are plenty of *good* heraldic plates which are a pleasure to see and to study, but a far greater proportion of bad. Most modern heraldry, as shown in the com-

mon or garden variety, is as smoke to the eyes and
as vinegar to the teeth.

But I must not arouse the ire of the book-plate
collector; men are proverbially sensitive about
their hobbies. For a short time I was a collector
in a humble way, till I was surfeited with bald
unlovely armorials which I received as exchanges
for designs of my own, drawn chiefly for friends.
I kept my examples in little folios until they grew
to sufficient quantity to be weeded and placed in
a more permanent home. The largest of these is
reserved for merely heraldic plates, which seldom
emerge from their obscure retreat. It is labelled
" The Dust-hole," and contains, I believe, some
of the ghastliest specimens known. During this
brief period I had much correspondence with
collectors, for all are very ready to impart information and assist the tyro with their knowledge and
experience. The most interesting communications
I had were from Mr. William Robinson of Birken-
head, whom I have never seen. That he is a
man of taste is evident from his book-plate, a very
good decorative one, designed and engraved for
him by Mr. Sherborn. I sent Mr. Robinson copies
of a few designs of my own in exchange for his
plate, and was rewarded after some days by receiving from him two short MS. stories he had
written, the motives of which were supplied by

these designs. The stories pleased me so much, especially the second one, by their quaint conceit and pretty fancy, that I felt desirous to print them in these pages, and wrote to Mr. Robinson to ask his permission to do so. That permission was at once most pleasantly accorded. Mr. Robinson wrote in reply: " You are quite welcome to use the stories, or any part of them which may happen to suit your purpose. They were written to wile away an evening with some friends, and there was an end of them." Some of the remarks on the artist's work in the " Death " story are somewhat too laudatory. It is from no conceit or vain-gloriousness that they are allowed to remain. They could not be left out without injuring the tale.

Ex libris R. T. PRITCHETT.

Dick started off early one morning to the butts, his arquebus on his shoulder and powder-flask at his side. He had often gone there before, but had never been able to hit anything, not even the target. The rabbits used to frisk about, knowing that they were perfectly safe, because as Dick could not hit his target, he could not hit them. The birds at first were very frightened at the noise, and flew away, but at last settled down on the roof of the target, and every time Dick got ready to fire they cried out "Prick it," and as sure as they did so Dick missed; and then the birds peeped down at the target, and finding he had missed, rose up wheeling and turning about screaming "Spero," that is to say, "I hope" (for better luck), and the sound seemed to Dick like mocking laughter. Now, Dick had for crest a stag's head "erased" (that is, violently torn from the body) on a "torse" or twist of silk, with a branch of oak-leaf and acorn in its mouth, and although Dick vowed he had shot the stag under an oak tree, his neighbours firmly believed that he had either found it ready killed, or that he had lain in waiting in the tree and noosed it. Dick was sorely puzzled for a motto, but not having a dictionary, didn't know what word to use. This day, as Dick was at the butts preparing for practice, the rabbits frisked about and the birds chattered on the roof, rising and falling restlessly, some crying out mockingly "Prick it," and some "Spero." Then Dick put a power of stuff into his arquebus, and blew down it with all his might, until his cheeks nearly cracked. Quoth a neighbour, "What art doing, Dick?" and presently Dick, recovering breath, repeated mechanically what the birds were saying, "Spe-ro." Then Dick knelt down and took aim at the target, but could not fire, because the birds chirped and the rabbits turned somersaults; then he lay down on his stomach, and still the birds chattered and the rabbits frisked about, and as a last resource he lay down on his back and took aim, and the birds and rabbits stood quite still with their mouths open.   Then Dick

fired.   The result was terrible, for every bird and every rabbit lay dead.   Quoth Dick with a whistle, "Spero."   Then said his neighbour, "Take that for thy motto," and Dick did so.

Reference is made in the following story to a

book-plate which I drew for my friend the Rev.
Robinson Duckworth, the year before he became
a Canon of Westminster. We had known him
since we first settled in St. John's Wood; at one
time we were very near neighbours, he living in a

PERSEVERANTIA·

·ROBINSON DUCKWORTH·

house immediately opposite. He was then, as he
is now, as everybody knows, the incumbent of
St. Mark's, Hamilton Terrace. The design is an
adaptation of " St. Francis Preaching to the Birds,"
the picture which gained for me the Associateship
of the Royal Academy.

Ex libris H. S. MARKS.

Death is said to play some strange freaks, and it is recorded that once upon a time a great actor was impersonating him in a play, and held the audience hushed with fear; and when the play was

over, the actor retired behind the scenes to lay aside his robes and tinsel crown, when who should touch him familiarly on the shoulder but Death himself. "Don't tremble, my friend," said Death; "life is but a walking shadow, and is as easily put off as thy robes." Now, a long time after this

incident occurred, a time when people had grown
wise, and ceased to have wars, when they had found
out the germs of all diseases and their antidotes,
Death rose up one day, being dissatisfied for want
of something to do, and went to a great city where
vice and misery had formerly abounded, and thought
to have a harvest. The first place he visited was
a church, to see if men had grown more pious, and
on entering a little side-chapel dedicated to St.
Francis, he saw a figure kneeling; and going along
noiselessly, he discovered that it was an old woman
in prayer before a picture representing one habited
as a monk discoursing to a group of birds. The
birds seemed to Death more wrapt in the preacher's
discourse than any human congregation he had
ever seen, there being no gapers or sleepers among
them, while their naïve expression tickled his
fancy. His attention was, however, attracted by
broken words from the old woman, and as he peered
into her face, and found it coursed with deep furrows
and her hands worn and horny, he heard her say—

> "A pitiful poor woman, shrunk and old,
> I am, and nothing learned in letter lore."

Then he retired a step as she said—

> "I, thy poor Christian, on thy name do call,
> Commending me to thee, with thee to dwell,
> Albeit in naught I be commendable."

Then he retired a step farther, as she said—

> "O Jesus, thou most excellent comforter,
>   Who even of this our weakness craved a share,
>   And for our sake stooped to us from on high,
>   Offering to death thy young life sweet and fair—
>   Such as thou art, our Lord I thee declare,
>   And in this faith I choose to live and die."

Then there was silence, and when Death came back and peered into the old woman's face, he found that the wrinkles had all gone, that a beautified smile was spread over it, and that her last words were her *Nunc dimittis*, for the spirit had really fled. Death stepped back awe-struck at the power greater than his own which had command of life, and as he looked again at the picture, it seemed filled with radiance, and he noticed in a corner the letters of the painter's name, H. S. M. His frame quivered with a strange emotion, and he drew his robe around him and noiselessly retired. The world was at peace, and the lamp of life burned brightly for the rest of that day.

Many years afterwards, Death again grew dissatisfied for want of occupation, and on a particular day he put on a robe of motley with a cockscomb, as if he were going out for a day's jest, and whetted and made ready his scythe for a big harvest among the lowly things; then he laid aside the scythe, thinking he would like to lop down some of the

big trees, and taking up his axe he sauntered out
into the fields of Life to view them. On one he
saw a tablet hanging, and he laughed to himself,
thinking "the fool in his pride hath hung up the
shield of his forefathers to show the world his
race," and presently coming to the tree, he traced it
over for any marks which lovers might have made,
and found the tree shapely and well preserved but
getting old. Then taking down the tablet, he sat
on a ridge to con over the blazon, when to his
surprise there was nothing on it but three letters,
H. S. M. "Ah!" he exclaimed, "this man hath
no arms, and therefore shows that he relies on the
work of his own hands;" and Death made merry
over it, and called to the birds to see, but they
flew away in fear. Then a strange feeling came
over him, and he racked his brain to remember
where he had seen the letters before, and presently
there came back to him the recollection of the
picture of the preacher preaching, the birds listening,
the old woman praying, and he said to himself,
"The mortal who is endowed with power to move
humanity like that is greater than I." And, as
the strange emotion quivered through his frame, he
twitched his robe around him, rose up and replaced
the tablet on the tree, and went his way noiselessly.
The world was at peace, and the lamp of life burned
brightly for the rest of that day.

This little story, pretty and fanciful as it is, hardly expresses the idea I had in designing my book-plate, which was Death grinning at the vanity of the painter in supposing his name would be remembered by posterity. It was conceived rather in the spirit of Dürer and Holbein. Mr. Robinson has but followed the example of many a critic, who discovers ideas and meanings in a painter's work of which that painter never dreamed. Nevertheless, it could be wished that the collecting of book-plates led to more of writing so pleasant and fanciful, instead of to such arid antiquarian discussions as whether a sixteenth-century gentleman did or did not compose for himself an imaginary shield of arms —or whether Henry VIII. ever carried as a crest "a virgin surrounded by a halo, or rays of light."

My task is done. I lay aside the pen not without a sense of regret, for the task has been congenial. If clouded over here and there by sad memories of friends and relations that are no longer here, the recollections of my life are for the most part bright and sunny. Though I cannot lay claim to Horatio's philosophic virtue of taking "fortune's buffets and rewards with equal thanks," I have not, I hope, been "a pipe for fortune's finger to sound what stop she please." A sanguine temperament and generally excellent health have hitherto enabled me to bear the cares, the vexations, and disappointments of life with some approach to equanimity. Yet always present with me has been the reflection, though not in a maudlin or melancholy sense, that "the night cometh when no man can work."

THE END—LAUS DEO!

The Ballantyne Press

1796

Ballantyne & Hanson

Edinburgh & London

www.ingramcontent.com/pod-product-compliance
Lightning Source LLC
Chambersburg PA
CBHW030345270326
41926CB00009B/970